はじめに

現在、英語を生活言語としない諸外国の英語教育で
Language Teaching）という、母語を一切使わずに英語でコミ
教授法が中心となっている。本書の姉妹版Dear Learnersの「まえがき」にも記したように、我が国の英語教育界でも、日本語を一切使わずに英語でコミュニケーション活動を行う授業が注目されている。英語学習は、「可能な限り早期に始めるべき」と喧伝《けんでん》され、中学・高校の授業でも対人コミュニケーションを重視すべきだと指導要領で謳《うた》われている。確かに、音声面における母語話者に近いレベルでの習得は、「早ければ早いほど効果的」と言え、第二言語習得研究においても、その主張はデータによって裏付けられている。しかしながら、母語として習得できる「臨界期」（critical period）を過ぎてしまった以上、つまり、日本語が母語として脳内のlanguage faculty（言語機能）にプログラミングされてしまった段階では、それと同じプロセスで英語を習得できる状況は至難を極めるだろう。

本書は、数頁を開けばおわかりのように、便利な会話表現を覚えるためのものではない。4技能（listening/speaking/reading/writing）に資《し》すべく、「意味を掴《つか》み取る力」と「音を掴み取る力」の総合的向上を目的として書かれている。我々の日常生活は、英語で営まれていない。そうした非生活言語の力を高めるには、音読やシャドウイングを通じての強弱リズムと連続音の特徴把握、多読・精読による語感の鍛錬、「なぜそうなるのか？」を絶えず理解するための理論的アプローチのどれもが不可欠となる。換言《かんげん》すれば、非母語話者は、学習する外国語の音と構造を、母語のそれらと意識的に対比させながら学ばなければ、「前に進む」ことができない。文字、音韻レベルから文法体系（つまりは、思考体系）に至るまで異なる日本語と英語においては、尚更《なおさら》である。

本書は、これまでの姉妹版であるDear ClassやDear Learnersと同様、Reading Sectionsでは、題材をレベル別に分けた上で、チャンク（意味の塊）毎に前から読み下していく母語的スタイルを主眼とし、多様なトピックや種々のタスクを通じて、楽しみながら学習できる工夫が為されている。加えて、Listening and Speaking Sectionsでは、リズム、強弱、抑揚、連続音といった音声面でのポイントも学べる仕組みとなっている。Grammar Sectionでは、これまでの解説とは少し趣を変えながらも、楽しい例文とイラストを交えながら、その文法項目の中核イメージ（core image）を伝えるべく努めている。一人でも多くの読者にとって、本書が英語の生涯学習への端緒となってくれることを願って止まない。

末筆ながら、今回も著者たちの思いを忍耐強く聞き入れてくださった南雲堂編集部の加藤敦氏並びに中田敦士氏と、常に著者の思い出や心象風景を見事にイラストで描いてくださる湯川れい様に対して、この場をお借りして、深謝申し上げたい。

令和5年10月

著者代表　永本義弘

Table of Contents

Part I

<Reading Sections>

Table of Contents

<Speaking and Listening Sections>

Part II

<Grammar Section>

本書の使い方

本書は **Part I (Reading と Listening & Speaking)** と **Part II (Grammar)** で構成されています。更に **Part I** は **Reading 1** (初級者用)と **Reading 2**(中級者用)に分かれています。**Listening & Speaking Sections** は **Reading** 各テーマに関連する会話文で **Role Play** や発音練習をします。

Part II は、基本文法を踏まえた大学生向けの独特な切り口で、参考書としての使用をも念頭に入れた内容です。

Reading Sections

ここでは特に速読スキルを身に着けることを目標にしています。単語の **Notes** に関しては別途 **Word List** を用意していますので、精読時に語句の意味を確認できます。

Reading 1 ＜初級＞

- Warm up：トピックに関連する質問です。
- Reading Passage：本文を速読し **WPM** を測り、**Phrase Reading**（意味のまとまり毎に読む）をします。
- Reading Comprehension：
  - **(1) Scanning**　本文から必要な情報を素早く見つけ出します。
  - **(2)** 内容理解問題　以下の３パターンです。
    - **1. Main idea** の掌握
    - **2.** 詳細を問う問題
    - **3.** 正誤問題
  - **(3)** 単語の **Matching**
- Trivia Quiz Challenge：本文に関連するトリビアクイズです。

Reading 2 ＜中級＞

Reading 1 と同様の問題構成です。

- One Point Grammar：**TOEIC** 頻出の文法問題に戦略的に取り組みます。

Listening & Speaking Sections

- Tips：英語の発話や聴解スキルを身に着ける為の秘訣や必要な基礎知識を確認します。
- Exercise 1-2：**Tips** を念頭に置いた練習をします。
- Exercise 3: Role Play：ペアでの役割練習による実践的会話を体験します。
- Exercise 4: Summary：**Dictation** を実施し、会話の内容の要約文を完成させて、理解します。

Reading 力を高めるためのポイント

1. 速読する：**Phrase Reading**で、返り読みをせずに直読直解し速読能力を養います。
＊速読力を高めるために毎回**WPM (Words per Minute)**を記録します。計算方法は、
WPM ＝読んだ英文の総単語数÷読むのにかかった時間（総秒数）× 60

2. スキミングとスキャニングの練習をします。
a. 内容を大意把握します。
b. 必要な情報を短い時間で素早く見つけます。

3. たくさんの英文に触れ文脈上の文章表現に慣れましょう。

4. シャドウイングします。
Step 1 Eye Shadowing：
音声を聴きながらテキストの文字を目で追って黙読します。
Step 2 Vocal Shadowing（**Overwrapping** とも言います）：
音声と同時にテキストを音読します。

Reading Sections の学習の進め方

Reading 1

Task 1: 音声を聴き **2** つのシャドウイング **(Eye Shadowing, Vocal Shadowing)** をします。
Task 2: 息継ぎやポーズにスラッシュ (**/**) を入れて、**phrase** ごとに和訳します。

Reading 2

Task 1: 本文を速読して **WPM** を測ります。
Task 2: **Reading Comprehension** に答えます。
Task 3: **Phrase** ごとに読み、直読直解します。
Task 4: **Vocal Shadowing** を行います。

Part I

Unit 1

Can You Guess What These Creatures Are?
A Jewel Under the Sea

Warm up

1. Do you like outdoor activities? Which do you like better, the beach or the mountains?
   a. I like the beach. b. I like the mountains. c. I like both. d. I prefer to stay home.

2. Name three kinds of sea creatures.
   For example: whales
   1. ________________ 2. ________________ 3. ________________

Reading

02

These sea creatures are floating in tanks in Kamo Aquarium, Yamagata. They live in all of the world's oceans. Many emit beautiful light and look like jewels in the ocean. They are composed of 95% water and don't have brains. As a method of self-defense, some can break up into pieces but not die. If you touch them, you'll feel a slick surface. But, be careful, they can sting.

Guess what they are. Yes, they're jellyfish!

They have another name, Medusa. In ancient Greek mythology, Medusa was a gorgeous woman with jewel-like eyes and beautiful hair. Athena, a powerful goddess, turned Medusa's hair into poisonous snakes. The jellyfish's stinging tentacles are like Medusa's dangerous hair.

For some sea creatures, jellyfish provide a means of transportation and are a source of entertainment. Certain crabs, instead of calling a taxi, hop on jellyfish to move from place to place. And dolphins use their noses and tails to toss jellyfish around like footballs. (160 words)

Reading Comprehension

(1) 下の語群から適切なものを選び、英文を完成させなさい。

1. Many emit beautiful light and look like (   ) in the ocean.
2. These creatures are (   )!
3. Medusa was a (   ) woman with jewel-like eyes and beautiful (   ).
4. ① Certain (   ) hop on jellyfish to move from place to place.
   ② (   ) use their noses and tails to toss jellyfish around like (   ).

a. dolphins	b. gorgeous	c. footballs	d. hair
e. jewels	f. jellyfish	g. crabs	

(2) 設問に対する最も適切な選択肢を選びなさい。

1. What is the main idea of the passage?
   a. The dangers of sea creatures   b. Different types of jellyfish
   c. Interesting facts about jellyfish

2. What is the connection between jellyfish and Medusa from Greek mythology?
   a. Medusa was a type of jellyfish.
   b. A jellyfish's stinging tentacles are like Medusa's dangerous hair.
   c. Jellyfish are a favorite food for Medusa.

3. Which statement is true?
   a. Jellyfish are composed of 100% water.
   b. Jellyfish can break up into pieces but not die.
   c. Jellyfish use crabs as a means of transportation.

(3) 左の定義と合う語を線で結びなさい。

1. very beautiful or attractive	•	•	composed
2. to be made up of	•	•	emit
3. to release or give off something, usually gas, light or heat	•	•	gorgeous

Trivia Quiz Challenge

1. T / F A Japanese scientist won the Nobel Prize for his research on a kind of jellyfish.
2. T / F There are no jellyfish fossils.
3. T / F Jellyfish help to clean up the sea.

Unit 2 An Innovation from Japan!

Warm up

1. Name three famous Japanese inventors.
   1. ________________ 2. ________________ 3. ________________

2. What are their inventions?
   1. ________________ 2. ________________ 3. ________________

Reading

03

Did you know that QR codes were invented by a Japanese company? They are on magazines, posters, billboards, and other media and make it possible to quickly access mobile websites. Incidentally, QR is an acronym for Quick Response.

QR codes were first distributed in Japan, but today they can be found all over the world.

Aichi-based DENSO WAVE received a request to include more information in a code. A DENSO WAVE team that had developed barcode readers created a 2-D code that could read large amounts of information at high speed. DENSO WAVE President Hara's idea for the QR design came from a Go board. In 1994, they issued their QR code, which stores 200 times more information than a barcode.

DENSO WAVE hasn't enforced its patent rights because the team wants the technology to spread around the world. In recent years, new ideas have emerged, such as a security-oriented QR code that can only be read by certain readers. Keep your eyes on the ever-changing QR code! (168 words)

Reading Comprehension

(1) 下の語群から適切なものを選び、英文を完成させなさい。

1. QR is an (　　　) for Quick Response.
2. QR codes were first distributed in (　　　).
3. QR codes can (　　　) 200 times more information than a (　　　).
4. DENSO WAVE hasn't enforced its patent (　　　) because the team wants the technology to (　　　) around the world.

a. store	b. Japan	c. acronym
d. spread	e. barcode	f. rights

(2) 設問に対する最も適切な選択肢を選びなさい。

1. What is the main idea of the passage?
   a. The history of QR codes and their invention by a Japanese company
   b. The technical details of QR codes and their advantages over barcodes
   c. The future possibilities of QR codes, including security-oriented codes

2. Where did DENSO WAVE's President Hara get his idea for the QR design?
   a. From a magazine　　b. From a Go board　　c. From a barcode

3. Which statement is true?
   a. QR codes are only found on magazines.
   b. QR codes and barcodes have the same capacities.
   c. DENSO WAVE hasn't enforced its patent rights for QR codes.

(3) 左の定義と合う語を線で結びなさい。

1. a large outdoor board used for advertising	•	•	acronym
2. to create something that has never been made before	•	•	billboard
3. a word formed from the first letter of each word in a phrase	•	•	invent

Trivia Quiz Challenge:

1. Who invented barcodes?
   a. Two British postgraduates　　b. Two American graduates
   c. Two Japanese undergraduates

2. What is the smallest QR code?
   a. 3.57mm×3.57mm　　b. 5.25mm×5.25mm　　c. 15mm×15mm

3. What did genius physicist Einstein call the "greatest invention of mankind"?
   a. Special Theory of Relativity　　b. compound interest　　c. QR codes

Unit 3 Moomin House Café

Warm up

1. What is your favorite cartoon character?
   I like ______________________________.

2. The Moomins are from (   ).
   a. Sweden   b. Finland   c. Norway

Reading

04

Some people may feel uncomfortable dining alone and may refuse to enter a café or restaurant without a companion. One Japanese café has found a novel way to help combat loneliness—large, stuffed Moomin dolls.

At a Moomin House Café, lone customers are seated with Moomins, hippo-like cartoon characters designed by Finnish illustrator, Tove Jansson.

Waitstaff add the stuffed animals to each table so all customers, whether solo or in a group, can interact with the various Moomins.

The café's popularity is now surging. On weekends, customers line up for the opportunity to dine on Moomin-shaped snacks and pastries and on bread made from Finnish rye. Though the café opened in 2003, it didn't gain fame and crowds of customers until "its 'loner-friendly' concept went viral." Your best chance for a seat? Try early weekday mornings.

The year 2014 marked the 100th anniversary of the birth of Tove Jansson. And in 2019, a Moomin theme park opened in Saitama. With all the special events associated with Moomins and their creator, it's likely the Moomin House Cafés will thrive again.   (180 words)

Reading Comprehension

(1) 下の語群から適切なものを選び、英文を完成させなさい。

1. A café has found a novel way to help combat (   )—large, (   ) Moomin dolls.
2. Moomins are hippo-like (   ) characters designed by a Finnish illustrator.
3. All customers, whether (   ) or in a group, can (   ) with the various Moomins.
4. On weekends, (   ) line up to (   ) on Moomin-related foods.
5. The year 2014 marked the 100th (   ) of the birth of Tove Jansson.

a. loneliness	b. dine	c. interact	d. anniversary
e. solo	f. cartoon	h. stuffed	i. customers

(2) 設問に対する最も適切な選択肢を選びなさい。

1. What is the main idea of the passage?
   a. The popularity of Finnish rye bread in Japan
   b. The history of Tove Jansson's Moomin characters
   c. The success of the Moomin House Café's "loner-friendly" concept

2. What is the best time to visit the Moomin House Café to avoid long lines?
   a. Weekday mornings b. Weekday evenings c. Weekends

3. Which statement is true?
   a. All customers, whether solo or in a group, can interact with Moomin.
   b. The café's popularity surged just after it opened.
   c. 2014 marked the 100th anniversary of the death of Tove Jansson.

(3) 左の定義と合う語を線で結びなさい。

1. a person or animal that spends time with another • • anniversary
2. a date on which a special event took place • • opportunity
3. a chance to do something • • companion

Trivia Quiz Challenge

1. T / F "The Moomins" were originally from comics.
2. T / F Moominmamma of the Moomins always carries her hat.
3. T / F Their family name, Trolls, was taken from an imaginary monster in Northern Europe.

Unit 4 Google's Happy Mistake

Warm up

1. What search engine do you use when surfing the Internet?
   I usually use ____________________.

2. Are you interested in new Japanese words? Do you know any new words or phrases?
   For example: emoi
   1. ____________________ 2. ____________________ 3. ____________________

Reading

05

Students around the globe "google" information on the Internet for their schoolwork. In fact, "guguru" is the Japanese word for "look it up on Google." But do you know how Google got its name?

In 1997, two Ph.D. students at Stanford University, Larry Page and Sergey Brin, were working on a search engine and named their newly completed product "Googol."

Googol is a mathematical unit that expresses 10 to the hundredth power. The two inventors named their product "Googol" because the search engine provides a huge amount of data like the "googol." But due to a spelling error during registration, the name ended up as "Google." In 2006, "Google" was included as a verb in the *Oxford English Dictionary.* If there had been no mistake, we would have "googoled."

One more bit of trivia: Google has hidden commands. Search for "askew" in Google, and the screen will be slanted. And if you search for "do a barrel roll," .... Guess what happens. Try it! (164 words)

Reading Comprehension

（1）下の語群から適切なものを選び、英文を完成させなさい。

1. Students around the globe "google" (　　　) on the (　　　) for their schoolwork.
2. Two men were working on a search (　　　) and named the (　　　) "Googol."
3. "Googol" is a mathematical (　　　) that expresses 10 to the (　　　) power.
4. If you search for "do a barrel (　　　)" in Google, you will be surprised.

a. unit	b. product	c. engine	d. roll
e. information	f. Internet	g. hundredth	

（2）設問に対する最も適切な選択肢を選びなさい。

1. What is the main idea of the passage?
   a. The meaning of the Japanese word "guguru"
   b. The history of Google's name and its hidden commands
   c. The success of Google as a search engine

2. Why did Larry Page and Sergey Brin choose the name "Googol" for their search engine?
   a. It means "to look it up on Google."
   b. It's a mathematical unit that represents a huge amount of data.
   c. They misspelled the word "Google."

3. Which statement is true about Google?
   a. The word "googol" means to search for something on the Internet.
   b. Google got its name due to a spelling mistake during registration.
   c. The term "Google" was included as a verb in the Oxford English Dictionary in 1997.

（3）左の定義と合う語を線で結びなさい。

1. to try to find something by seeking carefully	•	•	inventor
2. to slope or lean in a particular direction	•	•	search
3. a person who creates or designs new inventions	•	•	slant

Trivia Quiz Challenge:

日本語のように聞こえる外国語があります。それぞれどの言語かを答えなさい。

1. taverna《タベルナ》 (　　)　　2. suigara《スイガーラ》 (　　)　　3. avo《アホ》 (　　)
4. sotalan《シオタラン》 (　　)　　5. alamak《アラマー》 (　　)

a. Arabic　　b. Malay　　c. Hungarian　　d. Spanish　　e. Italian

Unit 5 Tasty Insects Save the Earth

Warm up

1. Japanese tea, Oolong tea, and Indian tea are all from the leaves of tea trees.
   a. Yes　　b. No

2. What are not commonly thought of as major delicacies in the world?
   a. truffles　　b. caviar　　c. crickets

Reading

06

Crickets and other insects have recently been featured in the media as "the food of the future." In fact, recipes using insects abound on online cooking sites. Why are foods made with insects booming?

The FAO* has regarded insect diets as a source of protein. Insect diets help combat the food crisis caused by global population growth. The WEF* has reported that insects could become an alternative source of protein that slows climate change. Insects emit almost no methane, a greenhouse gas emitted by livestock that is considered one of the causes of global warming.

In Japan, the University of Tokushima has been conducting research on crickets as a food source since 2016. MUJI has also used crickets as "an opportunity to think about food shortages and environmental issues" and as "one of the foods rich in protein." They launched cricket crackers in 2020 and cricket chocolate in 2021. Recently, Minister Taro Kono tasted the dried crickets at a venture company presentation and praised the crickets as "delicious, irresistible, and light." Soon after, "Cricket Taro" became a trending topic on Twitter (now X).

In sum, insect diets are nutritious and environmentally friendly. The secret to eating insects? You should not remember the foods' original form.　(205 words)

*FAO: The Food and Agriculture Organization of the United Nations　国際連合食糧農業機関
*WEF: The World Economic Forum　世界経済フォーラム

Reading Comprehension

(1) 下の語群から適切なものを選び、英文を完成させなさい。

1. Recipes using (　　　) abound on online cooking (　　　).
2. Insects (　　　) almost no methane, a greenhouse gas emitted by (　　　).
3. Minister Taro Kono (　　　) the crickets as "delicious, irresistible, and light."
4. Insect diets are (　　　) and (　　　) friendly.

a. emit	b. environmentally	c. sites	d. praised
e. nutritious	f. insects	g. livestock	

(2) 設問に対する最も適切な選択肢を選びなさい。

1. What is the main idea of the passage?
   a. Crickets are becoming more popular in Japan.
   b. Insect-based diets can combat food shortages and help the environment.
   c. Insects emit almost no methane, a greenhouse gas emitted by livestock.

2. What is the WEF's report on insects as a protein source?
   a. Insects emit more methane than livestock.
   b. Insects are a threat to the environment.
   c. Insects could be an alternative source of protein that slows climate change.

3. Which statement is true?
   a. Recipes using insects can only be found in special cooking books.
   b. Insects are being promoted in the media as a food for the future.
   c. Insects emit a large amount of methane, which causes global warming.

(3) 左の定義と合う語を線で結びなさい。

1. a place where a particular event or activity is occurring •		• emit
2. send out something such as light, heat, gas, etc •		• alternative
3. one of two or more available possibilities •		• site

Trivia Quiz Challenge

1. Where are cricket's ears?　　a. head　　b. forefeet　　c. rear legs

2. How many people will face food insecurity in the world in 2023?
   a. 8 million people　　b. 170 million people　　c. 333 million people

3. Which European country has the most widespread insect diets?
   a. Italy　　b. Finland　　c. the U.K.

Unit 6 A Man Picking Up Luck

Warm up

1. Do you like to play sports?

   Yes, → What sports do you like best?

   —I like ______________________________.

   No, → Why not? Tell me more.

   —______________________________

2. Do you have any favorite Japanese baseball players?

   Yes, → ______________________________ is my favorite player.

   No, → but I'm interested in ______________________________.

Reading

07

Good manners and respect are just as important as homeruns and strikeouts in Japanese baseball culture. Players take off their caps as they enter and exit the field and give full effort for their fans and teammates. All-Star player Shohei Ohtani epitomizes the best of Japanese baseball culture.

Ohtani treats his fans, the umpires and ball boys and ball girls courteously. For example, he devotes much of his time to autographing fans' souvenirs. He also has a unique habit while on the baseball diamond; he picks up trash!

Ohtani's unusual habit started in high school. His high school coach claimed that players who drop trash were dropping bits of luck. So, if Ohtani picked up the trash, he would collect the luck. Even after achieving great fame, Ohtani continues to pick up trash on MLB diamonds.

Respect and good manners have certainly helped Ohtani to become a superstar player. (149 words)

Reading Comprehension

(1) 下の語群から適切なものを選び、英文を完成させなさい。

1. Players take off their caps and give full (　　　) for their fans and teammates.
2. He also has a unique (　　　) while on the baseball diamond; he picks up (　　　)!
3. His high school (　　　) claimed that players who drop trash were dropping (　　　).
4. Respect and good manners have certainly helped Ohtani to become a (　　　) player.

a. coach	b. trash	c. superstar
d. luck	e. effort	f. habit

(2) 設問に対する最も適切な選択肢を選びなさい。

1. What is the main idea of the passage?
   a. Shohei Ohtani is a great baseball player in Japan.
   b. Good manners and respect are important in Japanese baseball culture, and Shohei Ohtani epitomizes them.
   c. Shohei Ohtani's habit of picking up trash brings him luck.

2. Why does Ohtani pick up trash on the baseball diamond?
   a. To impress his fans　　b. To show respect to the umpires　　c. To collect luck

3. Which statement is true?
   a. Ohtani treats his fans, the umpires, and ball boys and ball girls discourteously.
   b. Ohtani's habit of picking up trash on the baseball diamond started in high school.
   c. Respect and good manners did not contribute to Ohtani's success as a player.

(3) 左の定義と合う語を線で結びなさい。

1. the state of being known or recognized by many people	•	•	epitomize
2. to sign one's name, especially in handwriting	•	•	autograph
3. to be a perfect example of something	•	•	fame

Trivia Quiz Challenge

1. The first Japanese MLB Hall of Famer is ______.
   a. Hideki Matsui　　b. Hideo Nomo　　c. Ichiro

2. Shohei Otani's father named him after ______.
   a. Yoshitsune Minamoto　　b. Kiyomori Taira　　c. Narihira Ariwara

3. Shohei Otani likes animation. What TV animation has he appeared in? ______
   a. Detective Conan　　b. Sazae-san　　c. Crayon Shin-chan

Unit 7 A Short History of Harvard University

Warm up

1. What do you enjoy about your college life?

2. What are you planning to do while you are in college?

Reading

08

Harvard University is located in Cambridge, Massachusetts, U.S.A. Founded in 1636, Harvard is the oldest university in America. Many famous people have taught at, studied at or graduated from Harvard, including eight U.S. presidents, 188 living billionaires and about 160 Nobel Laureates. Harvard University Library is the oldest library in America and the largest private library system in the world. Its 80 library buildings contain 20 million volumes. Harvard also has many museums under its control. For example, the Fogg Museum contains priceless works by Van Gogh, Picasso and many other famous artists. Studying at Harvard is very difficult; Harvard accepts only about 6% of the people who apply. International students make up over 25% of the students at Harvard's Graduate and Professional schools. To accommodate women, the university created the Harvard Annex in 1879. The Annex's first class consisted of 27 women. In 1975, Harvard adopted an equal admissions policy for male and female undergraduates. During the mid-2010s, Harvard received two cash gifts from alumni totaling $750 million to improve the Schools of Public Health and of Engineering and Applied Sciences. (182 words)

Reading Comprehension

(1) 下の語群から適切なものを選び、英文を完成させなさい。

1. Founded in 1636, Harvard is the (　　　　) university in America.
2. Harvard University Library's 80 library buildings contain 20 million (　　　　).
3. Harvard (　　　　) only about 6% of the people who (　　　　).
4. In 1975, Harvard adopted an (　　　　) admissions policy.
5. During the mid-2010s, Harvard received $750 million from two (　　　　).

a. volumes	b. apply	c. alumni
d. equal	e. accepts	f. oldest

(2) 設問に対する最も適切な選択肢を選びなさい。

1. What is Harvard University?
   a. The oldest university in the world　　b. The oldest university in America
   c. The largest university in America
2. When did Harvard adopt a gender-equal admission policy for undergraduates?
   a. 1879　　b. 1975　　c. mid-2005
3. Which statement is true?
   a. Harvard University was founded in the 17th century.
   b. Harvard University Library is the largest public library in the world.
   c. Harvard accepts about 25% of the people who apply.

(3) 左の定義と合う語を線で結びなさい。

1. having the same status, rights, or opportunities	•	• priceless
2. having a value that cannot be measured or calculated	•	• found
3. to establish or set up (an institution, organization, etc.)	•	• equal

Trivia Quiz Challenge

1. What was the percentage of students who went on to universities in Japan in 2022?
   a. around 27%　　b. around 37%　　c. around 57%
2. Harvard University is part of the Ivy League, an athletic conference composed of elite universities. How many universities are part of the Ivy League?
   a. 3　　b. 6　　c. 8
3. When was the oldest university in Europe founded?
   a. In the 9th century　　b. In the 11th century　　c. In the 13th century

Unit 8 Humanitude

Warm up

Suppose you meet an elderly person while walking in the street. He/She seems to be in trouble.

1. What will you do?

   Your answer: I will ______________________.

   a. pass by without saying anything.
   b. talk to the person and say, "What's wrong? Can I help you?"
   c. call someone else to help the person.

2. If you chose b, what is the best way to approach in order not to surprise the person?

   The best way is to stand ______________________.

   a. just in front of the person, smiling and waving
   b. behind the person so that they can't see you
   c. next to the person

Reading

09

Humanitude is a method of caring for people with dementia or other illnesses that focuses on the patient. Humanitude stresses understanding, connecting emotionally, and behaving ethically toward others. In nursing care, Humanitude concentrates on five principles: standing, eye contact, smiling, touch, and communication. For sick patients, it's important to get them standing and walking as soon as possible to improve circulation. Warm visual eye contact attracts the patients' attention and provides them with a sense of dignity. Smiling helps nervous patients feel at ease. Touch provides warmth, reassures, and comforts the sick. Communication can convey the hope of getting better, inform and encourage patients. Using these principles can improve patient care and inspire caregivers. (114 words)

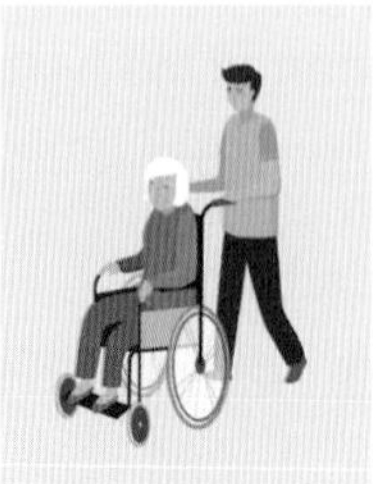

Reading Comprehension

(1) 下の語群から適切なものを選び、英文を完成させなさい。

1. Humanitude is a method of caring for people with (   ) or other illnesses.
2. Humanitude has five principles:
   ① To get patients standing and walking as soon as possible to improve (   ).
   ② Warm visual eye contact provides patients with a sense of (   ).
   ③ Smiling helps nervous patients feel at (   ).
   ④ Touch provides warmth, reassures, and (   ) the sick.
   ⑤ Communication can (   ) the hope of getting better.
3. These principles can improve patient care and (   ) caregivers.

a. circulation	b. ease	c. inspire	d. convey
e dignity	f. comforts	g. dementia	

(2) 設問に対する最も適切な選択肢を選びなさい。

1. What is the main idea of the passage?
   a. The importance of human connection in healthcare
   b. The principles of Humanitude in nursing care
   c. The role of communication in inspiring caregivers
2. Which of the following is NOT a principle of Humanitude?
   a. Communication　　b. Medication　　c. Touch
3. What does Humanitude focus on?
   a. Caring for caregivers　　b. Caring for the environment　　c. Caring for patients

(3) 左の定義と合う語を線で結びなさい。

1. the movement of blood through the body　•　　• patient
2. a person who receives medical attention, care, or treatment　•　　• dignity
3. the state of being worthy of honor or respect　•　　• circulation

Trivia Quiz Challenge

1. T / F　To prevent dementia, we should drink alcohol alone.
2. T / F　To prevent dementia, we should read magazines and newspapers aloud.
3. T / F　To prevent dementia, we should keep a diary and make our memory work actively.

Unit 9 Tree of Wisdom

Warm up

1. Do you like tea or coffee?
   I like ____________________. (or) I prefer to drink ____________________.

2. Do you go to cafés? — I ________ go to cafés.
   a. often b. sometimes c. seldom d. never

Reading

10

Coffee is one of the most popular drinks in the world. One reason for its popularity is the energy boost we get from the caffeine in coffee. But do you know why coffee plants contain caffeine? Because caffeine acts as a pesticide! Insects that try to eat the leaves, berries or other parts of the plant may be paralyzed or killed by the caffeine. Yet the coffee plants have flowers and need bees to pollinate them. Wouldn't the caffeine kill the bees too? Actually, no. It seems the caffeine, in low doses, helps the bees "remember, and return to, flowers which contain caffeine." If the bees better remember where the flowers are located, then they're more likely to return and help pollination. So both species benefit—the coffee plants are pollinated and the bees receive a caffeine boost! (138 words)

Reading Comprehension

(1) 下の語群から適切なものを選び、英文を完成させなさい。

1. One reason for coffee's popularity is the energy (　　　) we get from the (　　　).
2. The coffee plants have flowers and need (　　　) to pollinate them.
3. The caffeine, in low (　　　), helps the bees remember and return to (　　　).
4. Both species (　　　): the plants are (　　　) and the bees receive a boost.

a. bees	b. flowers	c. benefit	d. caffeine
e. doses	f. pollinated	g. boost	

(2) 設問に対する最も適切な選択肢を選びなさい。

1. What is the main idea of the passage?
   a. Bees and coffee plants have a beneficial relationship.
   b. Coffee plants are dangerous to bees.
   c. Coffee is the most popular drink in the world.

2. Why do coffee plants need bees?
   a. To produce caffeine　b. To help them grow taller　c. To pollinate the flowers

3. Which statement is true?
   a. Caffeine in coffee kills bees that help pollination.
   b. Insects that eat coffee plants are not affected by caffeine.
   c. In low doses, caffeine helps bees remember and return to flowers.

(3) 左の定義と合う語を線で結びなさい。

1. a quantity of a medicine or drug taken at a particular time ・		・ pesticide
2. a substance used for killing insects harmful to plants or animals ・		・ species
3. a group of living organisms consisting of similar individuals ・		・ dose

Trivia Quiz Challenge

1. T / F　You can order an "American Coffee" in the U.S.
2. T / F　Bach composed a comic opera, "Coffee Cantata."
3. T / F　Turkish coffee is a World Intangible Cultural Heritage.

Unit 10 Mysterious Antarctica

Warm up

1. Where do penguins live?
   a. around the Southern Ocean b. around the Arctic Ocean c. around the Pacific Ocean

2. What was the lowest recorded temperature on Earth?
   a. -41℃ b. -53℃ c. -89℃

Reading

11

Would you visit a place that has only two seasons, summer and winter? What if summer in this place was always sunny and winter was always dark? Would you still be interested? If so, head to Antarctica.

Antarctica is the southernmost and coldest place on our planet. Antarctica is very dry, and it rarely snows. However, the snow that falls doesn't melt. Over time, this snow builds up and forms thick ice sheets. So, much of Antarctica looks snowy, white, barren and mostly flat. It is, of course, too cold for trees and bushes to grow, but there are moss and algae.

Visits take place during summer. Should you decide to go, you'd be one of only about 5,000 people on the entire continent! The population drops to 1,000 during winter. But if you need company, you can hang out with the estimated 40 million penguins and some of the researchers working to uncover the mysteries of Antarctica. (158 words)

Reading Comprehension

(1) 下の語群から適切なものを選び、英文を完成させなさい。

1. Summer in this place is always (　　　　) and winter is always (　　　　).
2. In Antarctica, it (　　　　) snows. However, the snow that falls doesn't (　　　　).
3. If you need (　　　　), you can hang out with the estimated 40 million (　　　　) and some of the researchers working to (　　　　) the mysteries of Antarctica.

a. company	b. sunny	c. melt	d. penguins
e. uncover	f. dark	g. rarely	

(2) 設問に対する最も適切な選択肢を選びなさい。

1. What is Antarctic's climate like?
   a. It has two seasons, summer and winter.
   b. It has four seasons with moderate temperature changes.
   c. It has only one season, which is always cold and snowy.

2. What kind of plant life can be found in Antarctica?
   a. Trees and bushes　　b. Moss and algae　　c. Grass and flowers

3. Which statement is true?
   a. It frequently snows in Antarctica.
   b. Trees and bushes can grow in Antarctica.
   c. The population of Antarctica decreases during winter.

(3) 左の定義と合う語を線で結びなさい。

1. a person or people, usually friends　・　　・ continent
2. one of the large land masses of the earth　・　　・ company
3. roughly calculate or judge the value, number, or quantity　・　　・ estimate

Trivia Quiz Challenge

1. How many species of penguins are there in the world?
   a. 6　　b.12　　c.18

2. Which is saltier?
   a. The Arctic Ocean　　b. The Antarctic Ocean

3. What is the name of the Japanese Antarctic observation ship from 2023?
   a. Souya　　b. Shirase　　c. Fuji

Unit 1 Paul and the World Cup

Reading

12

The odds of correctly choosing the winner of Germany's 2010 World Cup matches was one in 256. But Paul, a common octopus, went 8-0 in his predictions.

Paul began his career guessing the outcomes of soccer matches during Euro 2008. His caretakers at the Oberhausen aquarium in Germany gave him a choice of two glass boxes. Inside one box was a picture of the German flag and in the other was the flag of Germany's opponent for the match. Each box contained a mussel, Paul's favorite food. Paul chose the winner by opening one of the two boxes and eating the mussel. For Euro 2008, Paul had a modest record of correct predictions at four out of six.

In 2010, Paul built on his experience and began predicting Germany's World Cup matches. With each correct prediction, his fame grew. Soon, Paul's predictions were broadcast on live TV and featured on social media. For Germany's semifinal match, Paul upset his German fans by correctly predicting that Spain would beat Germany. Some German supporters then suggested Paul be thrown into a frying pan!

A few months after the World Cup, Paul died. His death left Germans saddened and prompted *Der Spiegel* to write a moving obituary about the clever octopus. Paul's legacy lives on in an octopus statue at Oberhausen aquarium and in his last prediction—that Spain would defeat the Netherlands in the World Cup final. (235 words)

Reading Comprehension

(1) Scan each paragraph and write the correct words in the blank.

1. Paul went (   ) in his predictions.
2. Paul chose the winner by opening one of the two (   ) and eating the (   ).
3. Paul (   ) his German fans by correctly predicting Germany's defeat.
4. Paul's last (   ) was Spain would (   ) the Netherlands in the World Cup final.

(2) Select the best answer for each question.

1. What is the main idea of the passage?
   a. Paul correctly predicted the outcome of Germany's 2010 World Cup matches.
   b. Paul became famous for predicting soccer match outcomes.
   c. Paul was a beloved figure in Germany.

2. Why did some German supporters suggest throwing Paul into a frying pan?
   a. Because he predicted that Spain would beat Germany.
   b. Because he refused to make predictions for Germany's matches.
   c. Because he ate too many mussels.

3. Which of the following statements is true?
   a. Paul correctly predicted all of Germany's World Cup matches in 2010.
   b. Paul's fame peaked during Euro 2008.
   c. Paul's last prediction was Germany would beat Spain in the World Cup semifinals.

(3) Find the word in the text with the same meaning as the definition.

1. to declare or indicate in advance (p   )
2. something received from an ancestor or from the past (l   )
3. cause someone to take an action (p   )

One Point Grammar ***Subjunctive present 【In paragraph 3, line 5-6】***

Some German supporters then suggested Paul be thrown into a frying pan!

1. They suggested that she ••••• home for a while.
   (A) stays (B) stay (C) stayed (D) has stay

2. He ordered that the investigation ••••• continued.
   (A) is (B) was (C) be (D) has

Unit 2 Robots for Work and Fun

Reading

13

For over 50 years, robots like Atom Boy and Doraemon have fascinated Japanese children of all ages. This fascination continues with two robots of today: Pepper and Kirobo.

Pepper was introduced in 2015 by Softbank. Its cute face and curvy design welcome visitors to hospitals, schools and businesses in countries around the world. But did you know that Pepper also holds a Guinness World Record? During the coronavirus pandemic, professional baseball games were played in stadiums without fans. The Fukuoka SoftBank HAWKS tried to enliven the atmosphere by having Pepper robots cheer the team on. The team started with five Pepper robots, but during a March 2021 game, the robot cheering section expanded to 100 robots. Guinness recognized this achievement as the largest robot cheering squad.

Kirobo, “a robot astronaut,” was launched by the Japan Aerospace Exploration Agency (JAXA) on August 3, 2014, to work with astronauts living in the International Space Station (ISS). Kirobo arrived at the ISS “aboard an unmanned Japanese cargo ship to help scientists study robot-human interaction.” After meeting the astronauts, Kirobo delivered its first message, “... a robot took one small step toward a brighter future for all.” To experience Kirobo here on earth, check out Kirobo Mini, a palm-sized robot that Toyota says will enhance the way you live.

With charming robots like Pepper and Kirobo, we can look forward to many more fascinating years with robots. (233 words)

Reading Comprehension

(1) Scan each paragraph and write the correct words in the blank.

1. Robots have (   ) Japanese children, which leads to Pepper and (   ).
2. The SoftBank HAWKS tried to enliven the (   ) by having Pepper robots (   ) the team on.
3. ① Kirobo arrived at the ISS aboard an (   ) Japanese cargo ship to help scientists study robot-human interaction.
   ② Kirobo Mini is a (   ) robot that will (   ) the way you live.
4. With (   ) robots, we can look forward to many more (   ) years.

(2) Select the best answer for each question.

1. What is the main idea of the passage?
   a. The history of Japanese robots and their impact on children.
   b. The launch of Kirobo, a robot astronaut, to work with astronauts on the ISS.
   c. The continued fascination with robots in Japan, exemplified by Pepper and Kirobo.
2. What is Kirobo's purpose in the International Space Station?
   a. To work with astronauts   b. To deliver cargo   c. To study the atmosphere
3. Which statement is NOT true?
   a. Pepper robots can be found in hospitals, schools and businesses around the world.
   b. Kirobo is a robot astronaut that arrived at the ISS aboard a manned spacecraft.
   c. Kirobo Mini is a palm-sized robot that Toyota claims can enhance your life.

(3) Find the word in the text with the same meaning as the definition.

1. to bring and hand over something to people who receive it   (d   )
2. to set something in motion, typically a rocket or spacecraft.   (l   )
3. to make something more interesting or lively.   (e   )

One Point Grammar *Adjectival usage of participles* 【*In paragraph 3, line 1-3*】

Kirobo, "a robot astronaut," ... to work with astronauts living in the ISS.

1. Any managers ····· in enhancing their leadership skills are recommended to join.
   (A) interested   (B) interest   (C) interesting   (D) are interested
2. At the end of the meeting, all employees should receive the manual ····· the operation.
   (A) detailed   (B) detail   (C) details   (D) detailing

Unit 3 Creating an Icon: Mickey Mouse

Reading

14

In the final scene of this cartoon character's debut, he throws a potato at a parrot, smacking the parrot in the face. The character's rude behavior offended parents. Letters from the parents reached the artist, Walt, who then incorporated their criticisms into later stories. Walt transformed his character's mischievous ways and created a politer, kinder character that kids could look up to. In addition, the character's long, rat-like tail was shortened and his eyes were enlarged, evolving into the figure known around the world.

Mickey Mouse debuted in *Steamboat Willie* in 1928. This seven-minute animated movie not only introduced Mickey, it also used synchronized sound for the first time. Synchronized sound matches the onscreen images to the soundtrack.

A second charming character appeared in the film, Minnie Mouse. After plucking Minnie from a riverbank with a crane, Mickey played music for her, marking the start of their relationship. And if you're wondering, Mickey and Minnie are married, though their wedding hasn't appeared in any animations. Walt said they got married "in private life."

There is some mystery as to how Walt Disney and his partner, Ub Iwerks, chose the name Mickey. The men originally named the mouse Mortimer. One story contends that Walt's wife suggested the name Mickey instead; a second story claims Mickey's name came from a toy. However the duo came up with the name, they had created an icon. (232 words)

Reading Comprehension

(1) Scan each paragraph and write the correct words in the blank.

1. Walt incorporated parents' (　　　　　　) into later stories.
2. *Steamboat Willie* not only (　　　　　　) Mickey but also used (　　　　　　) sound.
3. Mickey plucked Minnie from a (　　　　　　) with a crane and played (　　　　　　) for her.
4. ① One story of the naming is that Walt's wife (　　　　　　) the name Mickey.
   ② A second story claims Mickey's name came from a (　　　　　　).

(2) Select the best answer for each question.

1. What is the main idea of the passage?
   a. Walt Disney's creation of Mickey Mouse and its evolution into an iconic character
   b. The debut of Mickey Mouse and Minnie Mouse in the animated film *Steamboat Willie*
   c. The mystery surrounding the origin of Mickey Mouse's name
2. How did Mickey Mouse meet Minnie Mouse?
   a. They were childhood friends.
   b. Mickey plucked her from a riverbank.
   d. Minnie saved Mickey from a trap.

3. Which statement is NOT true?
   a. Walt incorporated the parents' criticisms into later stories.
   b. Mickey Mouse debuted in *Snow White and the Seven Dwarfs*.
   c. Mickey and Minnie's wedding hasn't appeared in any animations.

(3) Find the word in the text with the same meaning as the definition.

1. a person or thing regarded as a representative symbol　(i　　　　　)
2. a pair of people, often working together or performing as a team　(d　　　　　)
3. to happen at the same time, particularly in sound and image　(s　　　　　)

One Point Grammar Gerund **(-ing) after preposition** 【*In paragraph 3, line 1-2*】

After plucking Minnie from a riverbank with a crane, Mickey played music for her ....

1. You must have a high proficiency in ▪▪▪▪▪ and basic computer skills.
   (A) type　　(B) typed　　(C) typing　　(D) to type
2. We look forward to ▪▪▪▪▪ your applications.
   (A) receive　　(B) receiving　　(C) receives　　(D) received

Unit 4　Etymology of the Word "Yabai"

Reading

15

Which translation do you use for " このケーキ、やばい "? This cake is super delicious or This cake is terribly bad? For the students in the classroom, it's probably the former, but for the teacher, it's likely the latter.

A 2014 survey* found 91.5% of 16- to 19-year-olds answered "delicious." Young people tend to use "yabai" to mean "very wonderful, delicious, cool." In contrast, 11.4% of those aged 60 or older and 18.2% of those in their 50s believe "yabai" meant "very wonderful, delicious, cool." Thus, "yabai" is overwhelmingly used in a positive, affirmative sense by the younger generation.

The word "yabai" has existed since the Edo period. At that time, prison guards were called "yaba." A popular hypothesis is that the adjective suffix 'i' was added to indicate a bad situation, where a criminal is about to be imprisoned in a yaba.

Since 1988, *Basic Knowledge of Modern Terms** has stated "yabai" means "dangerous." In the 2000s, the updated edition wrote that young people use "yabai" as a positive, nuanced word for "wonderful." *The Daijirin Revised* in 2006 added new definitions "amazing" and "a state in which one's feelings are severely shaken" as well as "dangerous." The new definitions of "yabai" have been carried over into *the Revised 2020, 4th Edition*. Now, "yabai" is recognized as an adjective with both positive and negative meanings.

Because it conveys many meanings, we tend to use "yabai" often. However, many people of a certain age use "yabai" only in a negative sense. So, if you do not consider your listener, you may end up being "yabai." (261 words)

* 文化庁〔国語に関する世論調査〕 Public Opinion Survey on the Japanese Language
* Basic Knowledge of Modern Terms 現代用語の基礎知識

Reading Comprehension

(1) Scan each paragraph and write the correct words in the blank.

1. "Yabai" means super (   ) and terribly bad.
2. "Yabai" is overwhelmingly used in a positive, (   ) sense by the (   ) generation.
3. "Yaba" meant (   ) guards in the Edo period.
4. In the 2000s, an (   ) dictionary wrote young people used "yabai" for "wonderful."
5. Many people of a (   ) age use "yabai" only in a (   ) sense.

(2) Select the best answer for each question.

1. What is the main idea of the passage?
   a. The different translations and meanings of the word "yabai"
   b. The history of the word "yabai"
   c. The positive and negative meanings of the word "yabai" and its usage by different age groups
2. What definitions of "yabai" were added in *the Daijirin Revised* in 2006?
   a. amazing   b. rude   c. cool
3. Which statement is NOT true?
   a. The younger generation overwhelmingly uses "yabai" in a positive sense.
   b. *Basic Knowledge of Modern Terms* has stated "yabai" means "dangerous" since 1988.
   c. Many people of a certain age only use "yabai" in a positive sense.

(3) Find the word in the text with the same meaning as the definition.

1. agreeing with a statement or to a request (a   )
2. to an extremely great extent (o   )
3. the origin and history of a particular word (e   )

One Point Grammar ***Tense 【In paragraph 3, line 1】***

The word "yabai" has existed since the Edo period.

1. This year's best-seller, World Entertainers, ····· positive reviews ever since it was published.
   (A) gets   (B) got   (C) will get   (D) has got
2. The portrait ····· a lot of positive reviews from critics since that time.
   (A) receives   (B) received   (C) has received   (D) will receive

Unit 5 Poison Gas?

Reading

16

Guess this mystery food. If you have ever smelled this fruit, you're unlikely to forget its unique odor. And it was this odor that nearly caused an international incident.

Looking for a taste of home, an Asian student living overseas went to a supermarket in Chinatown and bought this mystery fruit. He left the supermarket and headed down the street. Pedestrians turned and glowered at him. The student then boarded a bus. At first, the bus passengers moved away from the student to escape the odor. After a few more minutes, they bolted from the bus, and the driver called the police. The student, unaware of the commotion he was causing, reached his stop, got off, and went to his dorm. He left the fruit on a table in his dorm room and hurried off to class. Then the real trouble ensued.

Building managers got calls from the student's neighbors reporting that there was a poison gas attack. So, the managers called the police, and the police called the army. An army hazardous materials team* arrived quickly, evacuated the building, and sealed off the area. All that trouble for a fruit!

By now you may have guessed the mystery fruit—durian.

Durian isn't the only food to cause international misunderstandings. In New York, the Office of Emergency Management* often receives calls about clouds of "deadly caramel gas" blowing through the city. Once again, Asian food is the culprit. Methi, a sweet Indian vegetable, produces the clouds of gas during processing.

So, before calling the police to report a poison gas attack, make sure there aren't any Asian fruits or vegetables nearby! (271 words)

*an army hazardous materials team 軍危険物処理班
*the Office of Emergency Management 緊急管理局

Reading Comprehension

(1) Scan each paragraph and write the correct words in the blank.

1. An ( ) nearly caused an international ( ).
2. At first, the bus ( ) moved away from the student to ( ) the odor.
3. Building managers got calls from the student's ( ) reporting a ( ) gas attack.
4. The mystery fruit is a ( ).
5. Methi is an ( ) vegetable and produces the clouds of gas during ( ).
6. Before calling the police, you should confirm there aren't any ( ) foods nearby!

(2) Select the best answer for each question.

1. What is the main idea of the passage?
   a. Durian is a dangerous and poisonous food that can cause incidents.
   b. Certain Asian foods can lead to misunderstandings and cause panic.
   c. An Asian student caused an incident by bringing a fruit into his dorm.
2. What did the building managers do after receiving calls from the student's neighbors?
   a. They called the police. b. They sealed off the area. c. Both a. and b.
3. Which statement is true?
   a. The student intentionally caused the incident with the fruit.
   b. Methi is a vegetable that produces a unique odor similar to durian.
   c. Asian food has caused misunderstandings in different parts of the world.

(3) Find the word in the text with the same meaning as the definition.

1. a serious or violent event, such as an accident or an attack (i)
2. risky or dangerous, especially to health or safety. (h)
3. a person who is responsible for a crime. (c)

One Point Grammar ***during vs. while* 【*In paragraph 5, line 4-5*】**

Methi, a sweet Indian vegetable, produces the clouds of gas during processing.

1. The manager persuaded Ms. Coleman to go to the fair ····· a business trip.
   (A) from (B) during (C) with (D) while
2. A corporate merger was proposed ····· the two companies were having a meeting.
   (A) during (B) but (C) unless (D) while

Unit 6 Tragedy to Triumph

Reading

17

As 16-year-old teenager Yuzuru Hanyu glided around the rink on his ice skates, he figured it would be a typical day of figure-skating practice. Suddenly, the ground began to shake violently, the pipes below the rink burst, and the ice cracked. While still in his skates, Yuzuru sprinted out of the rink into the cold March air.

Yuzuru's hometown of Sendai was near the epicenter of the devastating earthquake on March 11, 2011. He and his family spent three days in a shelter because their home was badly damaged. The ice rink would remain closed for months. At that time Yuzuru couldn't imagine what joys he would experience in the upcoming Olympics.

Every day Yuzuru relived the quake and feared he might die. To improve his jumping ability, Yuzuru used visualization techniques. Instead of imagining how he would land his jumps, he saw the disaster. Yuzuru felt that things were beyond his control and said, "Everything exists just by luck."

Eventually his attitude changed and he gained a greater sense of purpose—to win the Olympic gold medal. Yuzuru wrote that "I want to make every day count now."

In Sochi in 2014, Yuzuru set the world record in the short program. A few days later, the gold medal was his. With the medal around his neck and joy in his heart, Yuzuru dedicated his victory to the people who suffered in the March 11th quake.

Four years later, Yuzuru repeated his Olympic feats with a gold medal at the 2018 Games. At the 2022 Games, Yuzuru skated on an injured ankle, yet still placed fourth. Yuzuru continues to show great compassion, determination and grace throughout his life and long skating career. (281 words)

Reading Comprehension

(1) Scan each paragraph and write the correct words in the blank.

1. Suddenly, the ground began to (   ), the pipes below the rink (   ), and the ice (   ).
2. Yuzuru and his family (   ) three days in a shelter after the earthquake.
3. Yuzuru (   ) the disaster when imagining how he would (   ) his jumps.
4. Finally, his attitude (   ) and he (   ) a greater sense of (   ).
5. He (   ) his victory to the people who (   ) in the March 11th quake.
6. At the 2022 Games, he (   ) on an injured ankle, yet still (   ) fourth.

(2) Select the best answer for each question.

1. What is the main idea of the passage?
   a. Yuzuru Hanyu's journey to become an Olympic gold medalist
   b. Yuzuru Hanyu's visualization techniques to improve his skating ability
   c. Yuzuru Hanyu's experience of the devastating earthquake and his triumph

2. What was Yuzuru's belief about luck?
   a. Luck is always on his side.
   b. Luck has nothing to do with success.
   c. Luck is beyond his control.
3. Which statement is NOT true?
   a. Yuzuru used visualization techniques to imagine how he would land his jumps.
   b. Yuzuru won a gold medal at the 2022 Winter Olympics despite being injured.
   c. Yuzuru dedicated his victory at the 2014 Olympics to those affected by the earthquake.

(3) Find the word in the text with the same meaning as the definition.

1. an achievement that requires great skill or courage (f   )
2. the central point directly above the earthquake's origin (e   )
3. happening or appearing in the near future (u   )

One Point Grammar ***Vocabulary (Verb)*** **【*In paragraph 5, line 3-4*】**

Yuzuru dedicated his victory to the people who suffered in the March 11th quake.

1.FBC Service is a consulting company that ••••• on marketing strategy.
(A) imports (B) puts (C) advertises (D) focuses

2. The leaflet says that taking photographs during the event is highly •••••.
(A) suggested (B) restricted (C) enclosed (D) allowed

Unit 7 The Power of Ideas

Reading

18

Time spent in Africa helped shape the views of two young Harvard University students, Julia Silverman and Jessica Matthews. While in Africa, the two experienced electricity blackouts and stayed in areas where electricity service was poor. Back at Harvard, Julia and Jessica teamed up to tackle energy problems in the developing world.

In a class called "Idea Transition Lab," they set out to create a product that could help generate electricity. Jessica and Julia remembered the smiling faces of the African children as they played soccer. And their idea was born—a soccer ball that could create electricity!

The first prototype soccer balls had problems. Some were too heavy and hurt your feet; others were too expensive to produce. The women thought they were in danger of receiving poor scores in their class. But they didn't give up on their goal. Eventually, they succeeded in producing a ball that was the proper weight, strong, and capable of producing electricity. They named it sOccket ball.

By now, former President Bill Clinton had learned of Julia and Jessica's sOccket ball, and he began to promote their invention. The exposure helped the women to send the balls to Haiti, Brazil, Nigeria, and Mexico. Once the sOccket balls have arrived in a community, Julia and Jessica work with NGOs and soccer teams to train customers how to use them. By working closely with the local communities, the women have created "a business model that allows them to help others, but also keep [their company] afloat."

When asked what motivated her to create the sOccket ball, Julia said, "It's about dreaming and thinking about your community and how you can better it through innovation." Good advice for all you young businesspeople.

(286 words)

Reading Comprehension

(1) Scan each paragraph and write the correct words in the blank.

1. Two women experienced electricity (   ) and stayed in areas where electricity service was (   ).
2. They set out to create a (   ) that could help (   ) electricity.
3. Some prototypes were too (   ) and others were too (   ).
4. They work with (   ) and soccer teams to train (   ) how to use the ball.
5. Their motivation was thinking how they can better the (   ) through (   ).

(2) Select the best answer for each question.

1. What is the main idea of the passage?
   a. Julia and Jessica created a soccer ball that generates electricity.
   b. Julia and Jessica faced challenges but succeeded in creating the sOccket ball.
   c. The sOccket ball is helping communities in developing countries.

2. The word “proper” in paragraph 3, line 4 is closest in meaning to
   a. light   b. pleasant   c. appropriate
3. Which statement is NOT true?
   a. Julia and Jessica experienced electricity blackouts in Africa.
   b. They created a soccer ball that could generate electricity.
   c. All the prototype soccer balls they produced were successful.

(3) Find the word in the text with the same meaning as the definition.

1. a first, original version of a product   (p   )
2. a new method, idea, product, etc.   (i   )
3. a temporary loss of electricity   (b   )

One Point Grammar ***Compound Nounsﾠ【In paragraph 1, line 3】***

... the two experienced electricity blackouts and ...

1. Travelers should know that ticket ----- are subject to change without notice.
   (A) price   (B) prices   (C) pricing   (D) priced
2. TGU Travel usually sends boarding tickets two weeks before ----- dates.
   (A) depart   (B) department   (C) departs   (D) departure

Unit 8 Humanitude in Action

Reading

19

The need for quality nursing home care is growing rapidly in Japan's aging society. New techniques to help nurses, caregivers and even patients' families provide the best care possible are necessities. One method of caring for the elderly, Humanitude, has begun to take root in nursing care facilities around Japan.

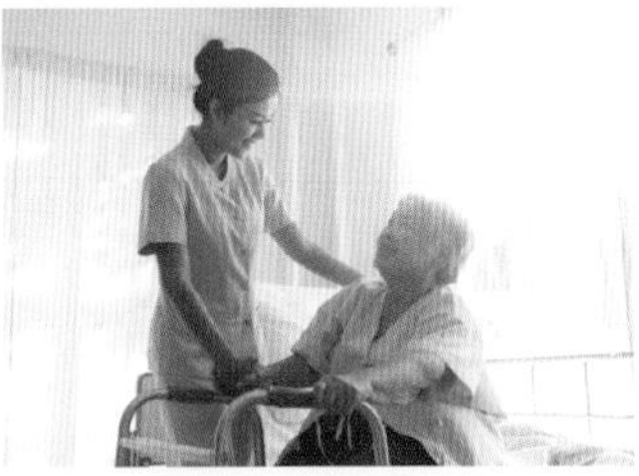

Humanitude was developed in France in 2000 by Yves Gineste and Rosette Marescotti. They created over 150 techniques to deal with sufferers of dementia compassionately. Their techniques are used in more than 400 hospitals and nursing homes in France.

Recently, Gineste visited a hospital in Tokyo to demonstrate Humanitude's method for dealing with dementia patients. After attending the demonstration, nurse Fuyuko Sekiguchi applied Gineste's method to a particularly challenging woman with severe dementia. Oftentimes, the woman would scream and resist taking a shower. When Sekiguchi used some of the skills she had learned, the woman "remained calm and even thanked" the nurse for her care, a reaction much different from before.

Fellow nurse Rika Tamura stated that caring for patients with dementia can be stressful, and that stress has caused many nurses to quit their jobs. But she added, "Workers may not have to quit if they know these techniques."

Skilled caregivers are in short supply in Japan. In a 2012 survey by the Care Work Foundation, 17% of caregivers quit their jobs annually, and "around 240,000 people are estimated to leave care work jobs in the country" every year. The Humanitude method not only improves care for dementia sufferers, but also may bring care workers more job satisfaction. (259 words)

Reading Comprehension

(1) Scan each paragraph and write the correct words in the blank.

1. Humanitude is a method of caring for the (   ).
2. Humanitude was developed in (   ) in (   ).
3. By using the skills, a patient with (   ) remained (   ).
4. A nurse stated that workers may not have to (   ) if they know these (   ).
5. Humanitude improves care for dementia (   ) and may bring care workers more job (   ).

(2) Select the best answer for each question.

1. What is Humanitude?
   a. A technique developed in Japan to improve nursing home care.
   b. A method developed in France to provide compassionate care for dementia patients.
   c. A program designed to train caregivers in Japan.

2. According to nurse Rika Tamura, why do many nurses quit their jobs?
   a. Due to workplace stress
   b. Due to poor working conditions
   c. Due to difficult patients

3. Which statement is true?
   a. Humanitude is a set of techniques for dealing with physical wounds in the elderly.
   b. Humanitude has been adopted by all nursing care facilities in Japan.
   c. The Humanitude method may bring care workers more job satisfaction.

(3) Find the word in the text with the same meaning as the definition.

1. to roughly calculate the number or quantity of something (e   )
2. to continue to exist or be present (r   )
3. to stop doing something (q   )

One Point Grammar **Passive Voice 【In paragraph 5, line 2-3】**

... around 240,000 people are estimated to leave care work jobs in the country every year.

1. Sales representatives of S&K Corporation ▪▪▪▪▪ to meet their clients at least every two weeks.
   (A) require (B) requires (C) is required (D) are required

2. The cargo ▪▪▪▪▪ last month, but it has not been delivered yet due to bad weather.
   (A) shipped (B) was shipping (C) was shipped (D) have shipped

Unit 9 Caffeine: More than Just an Energy Booster

Reading

20

Whether it's studying for finals, driving late at night, or recharging at work, millions turn to coffee, tea, or soda for a caffeine energy boost. Researchers now have another reason for you to consume caffeine—improved memory.

Michael Yassa, an assistant professor at Johns Hopkins University, led a team of researchers that looked at the effects of caffeine on long-term memory. The subjects first viewed a series of images. Five minutes later, they took either a placebo or a 200-milligram caffeine pill. Professor Yassa monitored the caffeine levels of the participants before they viewed the images and after taking the pills. He continued to monitor their caffeine levels at one-, three- and 24- hour intervals.

The following day, the two groups viewed a second series of images. The second series contained some images that were the same as the first series, some that were new, and others that were similar, but not the same.

Professor Yassa found that "more members of the caffeine group were able to correctly identify the new images as 'similar' to previously viewed images." The placebo group members, however, were more likely to misidentify the similar images as being the "same" as previously viewed images. Professor Yassa concluded that the ability to distinguish between two similar but not identical images "reflects a deeper level of memory retention." Caffeine seems to improve this retention.

So, if you're ever in a situation when you really need to improve your "deep level of memory retention," reach for that caffeinated drink! (251 words)

Reading Comprehension

(1) Scan each paragraph and write the correct words in the blank.

1. Besides an energy boost, (   ) can improve (   ).
2. The (   ) first viewed a series of (   ). Five minutes later, they took either a (   ) or a caffeine (   ). Yassa (   ) the caffeine levels of the patients before and after taking the (   ). He continued to monitor the caffeine levels at one-, three- and 24- hour (   ).
3. The second series of images contained three kinds: the same, the new, and (   ) but not the same.
4. This research shows that caffeine seems to (   ) memory (   ).
5. To improve memory retention, you should have a (   ) drink.

(2) Select the best answer for each question.

1. What is the main idea of the passage?
   a. Caffeine can help you study for finals, drive late at night, and recharge at work.
   b. Researchers have found that caffeine can improve long-term memory.
   c. Participants were given caffeine pills and tested on their memory the following day.
2. The word "previously" in paragraph 4, line 2 is closest in meaning to
   a. regularly   b. formerly   c. accidentally
3. Which statement is NOT true?
   a. Researchers found that caffeine can improve long-term memory.
   b. Participants were given either a placebo or a 200-milligram caffeine pill.
   c. Professor Yassa concluded that caffeine is the only way to improve memory.

(3) Find the word in the text with the same meaning as the definition.

1. a substance that has no effect to cure diseases (p   )
2. a person who is being studied, especially in an experiment (s   )
3. to increase or improve something, especially in terms of energy (b   )

One Point Grammar ***Part-of-speech (Adjectives)*** 【*In paragraph 4, line 5-6*】

... between two similar but not identical images "reflects a deeper level of memory retention."

1. According to the survey, most diners had positive opinions about our ▪▪▪▪▪ atmosphere.
   (A) cheer   (B) cheerful   (C) cheerfulness   (D) cheerfully
2. Bills' Kitchen has earned a reputation for ▪▪▪▪▪ and creative cuisine.
   (A) innovation   (B) innovate   (C) innovatively   (D) innovative

Unit 10 What Lies Below the Ice?

Reading

21

Antarctica contains 90% of the ice on Earth. And what lies below 800 meters of ice in Antarctica? Life. In 2013, scientists discovered microbes living in Lake Whillans, a large body of water underneath the ice of Antarctica. The discovery began with a long, difficult journey in the southernmost place on Earth.

From U.S. McMurdo Antarctic Station, a team of 50 scientists drove 12 days in 20 tractors with 230 tons of payload to reach Lake Whillans and establish camp. Once they had arrived, the scientists faced another challenge—how to reach the lake 800 meters below the ice. Their solution was to rely on a hot-water drill. This drill reduced the chances of damaging the environment and any samples obtained from the lake.

After the drilling was completed, the scientists sent down a probe, which had a camera that sent back live images of the lake. They then collected lake-water samples and used a mobile lab to test for the presence of cellular DNA. To the scientists' great surprise, they found "very good evidence" that showed there were not only cells in the water but that they were alive.

These life forms from the lake "have survived in a dark, cold habitat for at least 100,000 years." A microbiologist and member of the team speculates that these life forms may rely on a "unique ecosystem in which life doesn't depend on photosynthesis."

Research on the lake-water samples continues. Scientists feel that the lakes under the ice will help them to understand "the secrets of Antarctica's geology, climate change, and, maybe, to life in general." (265 words)

Reading Comprehension

(1) Scan each paragraph and write the correct words in the blank.

1. In 2013, scientists discovered (   ) living in Lake Whillans.
2. From U.S. McMurdo Antarctic Station, a team of (   ) scientists drove (   ) days in (   ) tractors and reach Lake Whillans and (   ) camp.
3. After the drilling, the scientists sent down a (   ), which had a (   ).
4. The microbes may rely on a unique (   ) where life doesn't depend on (   ).
5. The lakes under the ice could make clear the secrets of Antarctica's geology, (   ) change, and (   ) in general.

(2) Select the best answer for each question.

1. What is the main idea of the passage?
   a. The discovery of microbes living in Lake Whillans
   b. The importance of Antarctica's lakes for scientific research
   c. The unique ecosystem in Lake Whillans
2. How long have these life forms survived in the lake?
   a. one thousand years   b. one hundred thousand years   c. one million years

3. Which statement is true?
   a. The discovery of microbes in Lake Whillans was made by 20 scientists.
   b. The scientists used a steel drill to reach the lake below the ice.
   c. Lake Whillans is located 800 meters below the ice in Antarctica and contains life.

(3) Find the word in the text with the same meaning as the definition.

1. a biological community of interacting organisms (e   )
2. the fact that makes you believe that something is true (e   )
3. a means of solving a problem or dealing with a difficult situation (s   )

One Point Grammar ***Conjunction (once) 【In paragraph 2 , line 3】***

Once they had arrived, the scientists faced another challenge.

1. ▪▪▪▪▪ the tourist season begins, Trattoria Porte will extend its hours of operation.
   (A) Because   (B) Although   (C) Once   (D) During
2. My colleague forgot to attach a file to her e-mail ▪▪▪▪▪ she was in a hurry to leave the office.
   (A) if   (B) once   (C) though   (D) because

Unit 1 Differences between Japanese and English Pronunciation (Vowels)

Tips

第一言語の干渉（常に日本語の母音を子音の後に続けて挿入しないよう）に気を付ける。

e.g. ando ⇒ and

日本語：母音 あ、い、う、え、お のみ ＋ 子音（母音以外）

e.g. sutoraiku 子音の後に全てに母音が入る発音の仕方。

英　語：日本語の母音「あ・い・う・え・お」に近い音（短母音、伸ばす長母音、二個ある二重母音）＋ 子音（母音以外）

e.g. strike 子音連結で、母音は下線部の二重母音１箇所のみ。

Exercise 1

Listen to the audio. Choose one word which is pronounced differently from the others. 22

[ei] **create / name / aquarium / entertainment /tails / maintain / great / brains**

[ai] **remind / eye / bright / glide / time / invite / ancient**

[oʊ] **problem / going / both / so / show / opponent / opening / thrown**

*[ʊ] the short sound of [u]

Exercise 2

23

Pronounce "strike" in Japanese, and then listen to the audio to pronounce it in English.

Exercise 3 Role Play

Listen to the conversation between Yoshi and Hiro from the audio. Focus on the vowel sounds in each individual word and practice vocal shadowing. Then, pair up and take turns being Yoshi and Hiro to perform the conversation. When pronouncing words such as 'what', 'and', and 'but', be careful not to add the Japanese-like 'o' sound at the end.

Dialogue 1

24

Yoshi: What did you do last weekend?

Hiro: I went to an aquarium.

Yoshi: Really? Where?

Hiro: Shinagawa Aquarium. The dolphin show was really great!

Yoshi: Yeah, I love the dolphin shows. They're so smart and athletic. What other sea creatures do you like?

Hiro: Sharks, of course! I think they're so beautiful, and they help maintain balance in the ocean. And what sea creatures do you like?

Yoshi: I like sharks, too. But I prefer turtles. I like to see them glide through the water. And 'Crush' from *Finding Nemo* is my favorite character from the movie. Next time you go to an aquarium, please invite me.

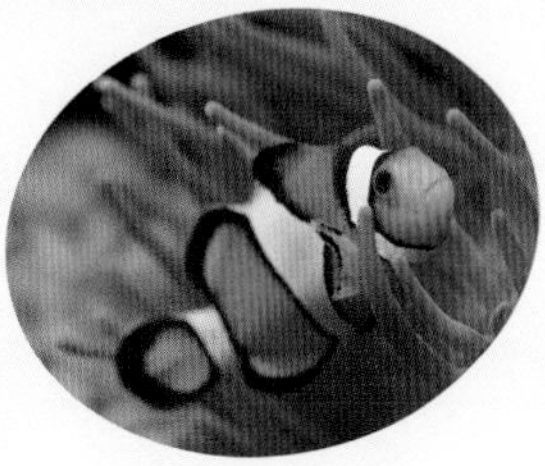

Hiro: Absolutely!

Exercise 4 Summary

Listen to the audio and complete the summary of *Dialogue 1*.
Work with your partner and discuss your answers.

25

Yoshi and Hiro are discussing their weekend (1.). Hiro went to Shinagawa Aquarium and enjoyed a (2.) show. They both like (3.), but Yoshi prefers (4.) because he enjoys watching them swim. Yoshi mentions 'Crush' from *Finding Nemo* as his favorite (5.). The conversation ends with an invitation to go to an (6.) together.

Unit 2 Consonants

Tips

注意すべき特に間違えやすく、**紛らわしい子音の違いに注意する。**

1. [r] **QR / receive / right / readers / recent / create / robots / respond / recorders**
   [l] **technology / billboard / large / level / allow / launched / delivered / largest**

2. [ð] **their / other / this / than / without / those / that / with**
   [θ] **think / thank / thousand / theory / anything**

3. [v] **five / develop / arrived / drive / visit**
   [b] **aboard / about / boat / best / buyer / Softbank**

4. [s] **space / station / sea / seat / single**
   [ʃ] **ship / shall / shock**

Exercise 1

Listen to the audio and practice the differences between consonants while paying attention to the underlined part. 26

live robots help introduced children country all around

play brighter largest recognize without think

thought school space ship arrive brighter

Exercise 2 Tongue Twister Challenge

Practice tongue twisters while being aware of the differences between [ʃ] and [s] in pronunciation. 27

She sells seashells by the seashore. How many seashells did she sell?

Exercise 3 Role Play

Listen to the conversation between Yoshi and Hiro from the audio. Focus on the consonant sounds in each individual word and practice vocal shadowing. Then, pair up and take turns being Yoshi and Hiro to perform the conversation, paying special attention to the pronunciation of consonant sounds such as *really*, *last*, *lessons*, *ride*, *trains*, *rush*, *record* etc.

Dialogue 2

28

Yoshi: I'm so tired of technology!

Hiro: Really? Why?

Yoshi: Well, I've spent the last few hours studying online with Zoom. It's not fun and I can't always see or hear what's going on. I wish I could study face to face.

Hiro: Not me! I love online lessons. I don't have to get up early and ride the trains during rush hour. And my teachers record their lessons, so if I miss anything I can go back and watch it again.

Yoshi: Yeah, but don't you miss meeting your friends and hanging out on campus?

Hiro: I do. But I can't spend much time on campus. I have to work. As soon as classes are over on Mondays, Thursdays and Fridays, I leave for work. And that's another reason why I like being online. I can get to work more quickly from my home than from campus.

Yoshi: I never thought about that. My situation is different. I've been a member of a dance circle since freshman year, and we used to practice every day on campus. We don't meet as often because of the pandemic.

Hiro: I guess everyone has their own unique reasons for liking or disliking online lessons.

Exercise 4 Summary

**Listen to the audio and complete the summary of *Dialogue 2*.
Work with your partner and discuss your answers.**

29

The two people focus on their differing opinions regarding (1.   ) learning. Yoshi is struggling with Zoom (2.   ) and wishes for (3.   ) learning because Yoshi can't meet friends. On the other hand, Hiro likes online classes for their convenience, (4.   ) of commute, and ability to (5.   ) recorded lessons. They also acknowledge that everyone has different (6.   ) for preferring or disliking online learning.

Unit 3 Linking (Liaison)

Tips

意味の繋がりがある際に子音 ＋ 母音の部分が連結されて発音される場合がある。（川の流れのようにつながっているイメージ）

e.g. enter a café / in a group / line up for / for a seat / without a

Exercise 1

Listen to the audio and underline the consonant and vowel linking parts in the following phrases. Pronounce them along with the audio. 30

1. **lone customers are**
2. **the stuffed animals**
3. **crowds of**
4. **the birth of Tove Jansson**
5. **and in 2019**
6. **with all the special events**

Exercise 2 Tongue Twister Challenge

Practice tongue twisters while focusing on the linked sounds. 31

I scream, you scream, we all scream for ice cream!

How much wood could a woodchuck chuck if a woodchuck could chuck wood?

Exercise 3 Role Play

Listen to the conversation between Yoshi and Hiro from the audio. Focus on the linking part of consonants and vowels and practice Sense Group Readings. Then, pair up and take turns being Yoshi and Hiro, paying attention to the pronunciation of the parts such as "on a," "seven of," "front of," and so on.

Dialogue 3

32

Yoshi: Some friends and I are going to Tokyo Disneyland. You interested?
Hiro: Absolutely! When?
Yoshi: Thursday morning. We're hoping it won't be too busy on a weekday.
Hiro: Thursday's perfect. What time?

Yoshi: Everyone lives in different places, so we'll meet in front of the gates at Maihama Station at 10:00.
Hiro: OK. And how many are going?
Yoshi: In total, there will seven of us.
Hiro: Sounds good. But what about the tickets? Should I reserve mine?
Yoshi: Yeah, that's the best option. Just go to the website and have the ticket mailed to your home.
Hiro: I will. And thanks again for the invitation.

Exercise 4 Summary

Listen to the audio and complete the summary of *Dialogue 3*.
Work with your partner and discuss your answers.

33

The conversation (1.) (2.) going to Tokyo Disneyland with friends. Yoshi invites Hiro, who enthusiastically accepts. They plan to go (3.) (4.) Thursday morning, hoping for less crowded conditions. They will (5.) (6.) Maihama Station at 10:00, (7.) (8.) total of seven people will be going. Hiro (9.) (10.) tickets and was advised to reserve them online and have them mailed to Hiro's home.

Unit 4 Reduction (1)

Tips

脱落：弱い音節が「nt」,「ct」,「st」に続く場合、その「t」の音が脱落する。

破裂音 [t] e.g. **printing** ＊特にアメリカ英語に見られる場合があります。

Exercise 1

Listen to the audio and read aloud while paying attention to the underlined letter. 34

winter / hunting / center / pointed / twenty / plenty

Exercise 2

35

Listen to the audio and underline the reduced parts.

The two inventors named their product "Googol" because the search engine provides a huge amount of data like the googol.

Exercise 3 *Role Play*

Listen to the conversation between Yoshi and Hiro from the audio. Focus on the reduction of consonants. Practice vocal shadowing. Then, pair up and take turns being Yoshi and Hiro, paying attention to the pronunciation of the parts such as *exactly, plenty*.

Dialogue 4

35

Yoshi: Hey, have you chosen a topic yet for your English paper?

Hiro: Not yet. I think I'll just Google something about sports and come up with an idea.

Yoshi: But Professor Tanaka said not to just rely on Google. She wants us to use the ideas in our brains and from academic research.

Hiro: I know. I won't use Google when I write the paper, just for ideas. So, what are you going to write about?

Yoshi: Well, you know I like movies and music, so I'm writing about famous movie theme songs, like in *Jaws*.

Hiro: Good choice. Even if you haven't seen the movie, you know the music.

Yoshi: Exactly. It fits the movie so well. And I got a plenty of my information from Google Scholar.

Hiro: Google Scholar? What's that?

Yoshi: It's basically a search engine, but only for academic articles. You should definitely check it out.

Hiro: I'll have to give it a try.

Exercise 4 **Summary**

Listen to the audio and complete the summary of *Dialogue 4*.
Work with your partner and discuss your answers.

37

They are talking about deciding on a topic for an English paper. Hiro is going to search for (1.) ideas on Google. But Yoshi reminds her that their teacher (2.) them (3.) (4.) just rely on Google. The teacher advised them to use their own ideas and (5.) research. Yoshi is writing about (6.) theme songs. Yoshi could find a lot of information on the topic using Google Scholar, which specifically targets academic papers. Hiro is thinking of trying it out because of the recommendation.

Unit 5 Flap

Tips

アメリカ英語における弾音：[t] が、有声化して [d] に近い音。日本語のラ行やダ行音に近く聞こえる。

e.g. water, butter, little

Exercise 1

Listen to the audio and underline the flapped sounds in 1-10 and then pronounce the words. 38

1. settle 2. forty 3. sitting 4. battle 5. bottle

6. not at all 7. put off 8. get out 9. it isn't 10. better

Exercise 2

39

Listen to the audio and underline the flapped sound [t].

... an opportunity to think about food shortages and environmental issues

It's cheaper to cook and I think the food is better for you.

Exercise 3 Role Play

Listen to the conversation between Yoshi and Hiro from the audio. Focus on the flap part of consonants. Practice vocal shadowing. Then, pair up and take turns being Yoshi and Hiro, paying attention to flap [t], as in better.

Dialogue 5

40

Yoshi: You want to grab some dinner tonight at the Indian place on the corner?

Hiro: I'd love to, but not tonight. I'm cooking dinner.

Yoshi: You can cook? Really?

Hiro: Yeah! I'm actually pretty good. My boyfriend's coming over and I'm cooking Italian food.

Yoshi: Spaghetti?

Hiro: No, no. Baked ziti. It's a pasta dish with meat and cheese. It's kind of like lasagna.

Yoshi: Oh. Sounds good. And how often do you cook dinner?

Hiro: Most nights. It's cheaper to cook and I think the food is better for you.

Yoshi: That's true. So, I guess I'll be dining at home then.

Hiro: Well, what are you cooking?

Yoshi: Me? Nothing! My mom's going to cook.

Exercise 4 Summary

Listen to the audio and complete the summary of *Dialogue 5*.
Work with your partner and discuss your answers.

41

Yoshi asks if Hiro would like to go to an (1.) restaurant for dinner, but Hiro declines because Hiro is cooking dinner at home for her boyfriend. Yoshi found out Hiro is actually (2.) (3.) at cooking and she is making baked ziti, which is a (4.) dish with meat and cheese. The conversation turns to cooking habits, with Hiro saying that she cooks most nights because it's (5.) and (6.). Yoshi decides to stay home for dinner and when asked what Yoshi is cooking, Yoshi says mom will be doing the cooking.

Unit 6 Contracted Forms

Tips

短縮形：口語における言葉を簡潔にするための音声的特徴。２語が縮約され一定の型となり、一語のように発音される。

Exercise 1

Practice the following contracted forms. 42

e.g. **I am → I'm, you are → you're, she is/she has → she's,**

he is/he has → he's cf. his,

there is → there's cf. theirs,

who is/who has → who's cf. whose,

had not → hadn't, let us → let's, shall not → shan't, do you → d'you,

will not → won't cf. want,

they are → they're cf. their, there

Exercise 2

Listen to the following passage and change the contracted forms into the original ones. 43

At that time Yuzuru couldn't imagine what joys he would experience in the upcoming Olympics.

Exercise 3 Role Play

Listen to the conversation between Yoshi and Hiro from the audio.
Focus on the contracted forms and practice vocal shadowing. Then, pair up and take turns being Yoshi and Hiro to perform the conversation, paying special attention to the contracted forms such as can't, there's, she's, she'll, couldn't.

Dialogue 6

44

Yoshi: Did you watch the Winter Olympics?

Hiro: Yeah, a bit. But I think I spent more time watching the Paralympics.

Yoshi: I only watched a tiny bit of the Paralympics. What event did you watch?

Hiro: Blind skiing! These skiers are amazing! Some of them reach speeds of 100 km/hour! Can you imagine going that fast and not being able to see?

Yoshi: No way! I had no idea they could reach those speeds. But how can they ski down a mountain if they can't see?

Hiro: There's a guide who skis ahead of the blind skier. The guide calls out information about the course and the blind skier follows the sound and advice. One blind skier said the scariest part is jumps and not knowing how high up she's jumped or when she'll land.

Yoshi: That's so cool! I've tried skiing only once. I was terrible at it and would be terrified if I couldn't see. I'll definitely have to check that out.

Exercise 4 Summary

Listen to the audio and complete the summary of *Dialogue 6*.
Work with your partner and discuss your answers.

45

The conversation above is about the Winter Olympics and Paralympics. Hiro mentioned watching the Paralympic (1.) skiing event and was amazed how they can ski without being (2.) to see. Hiro explains that there is a guide who skis (3.) of the blind skier and calls out information about the course. Hiro also mentions that (4.) are particularly (5.) for the blind skiers. Yoshi admits to having tried skiing only once and feeling scared if he (6.) see.

Unit 7 Rhythm (Stress-Timed Rhythm)

Tips

ワルツのような特徴の強勢のリズムで、文脈上機能語にアクセントを置く場合を除き、内容語に強勢を置いて発話する。

＊内容語（強く発音される語、主に、名詞、動詞、形容詞、副詞等）と、弱く発音される機能語（主に、冠詞、前置詞、代名詞等）がある。

Exercise 1

Listen to the audio and then practice pronunciation while paying attention to the triple meter rhythm for each slash. 46

Monkeys / eat / bananas.
● ● ●

The monkeys / eat / bananas.
● ● ●

The monkeys / eat / the bananas.
● ● ●

The monkeys / will eat / the bananas.
● ● ●

The monkeys / will have eaten / the bananas.
● ● ●

Exercise 2

Listen to the audio and then practice pronunciation, paying attention to each rhythm. 47

I suppose so.
○ ● ○

Where would you go?
● ○ ○ ●

Exercise 3 Role Play

Listen to the conversation between Yoshi and Hiro from the audio. Focus on the rhythm and practice vocal shadowing. Then, pair up and take turns being Yoshi and Hiro to perform the conversation, paying special attention to the rhythm.

Dialogue 7

48

Yoshi: You know, I was glad the professor talked about the time he spent studying overseas.

Hiro: Really? Why?

Yoshi: Well, I've been thinking about studying abroad. I think it would be fun to experience life in a foreign country.

Hiro: I suppose so. But there's so much to worry about with the virus and all.

Yoshi: I know what you mean. I wish I could just erase COVID-19 from the face of the earth!

Hiro: Me, too! But if you could study abroad, where would you go?

Yoshi: I haven't looked too seriously at going overseas yet, but I think New Zealand would be a great place to study and live.

Hiro: New Zealand?

Yoshi: Yeah, I have this image of New Zealand as peaceful and filled with beautiful nature. Also, I've met a few Kiwis, and they were all friendly.

Hiro: Well, how long do you think you'd stay, if you can go?

Yoshi: Good question. I guess I'd try to stay for a semester, and if I liked it, try to extend my stay.

Hiro: Sounds good. I hope it works out for you.

Yoshi: Thanks.

Exercise 4 ***Summary***

Listen to the audio and complete the summary of *Dialogue* 7.
Work with your partner and discuss your answers.

49

Yoshi is (1.   ) that his professor talked about his time studying (2.   ) because Yoshi has been (3.   ) studying abroad. Yoshi mentions New Zealand as a (4.   ) destination, as he sees it as a (5.   ) and (6.   ) place.

Unit 8 Stress, Pitch & Intonation

Tips

ピッチ（音の高低）によるイントネーション、発話の際に感情や態度を表現する為の文全体の声の上げ下げの調子が変化する。

Exercise 1

50

Listen to the audio and then practice pronunciation. Pay attention to pitch & intonation. Then, pair up and take turns being A and B.

1. **A: Where is the bike, Mike?** **B: It's at the park, Mark.**
2. **A: How's the food, Jude?** **B: It's really nice, Bryce.**

Exercise 2

51

There are four intonation patterns that depend on where emphasis is placed within the flow of conversation. Listen to the audio and add intonation lines (＿/￣)* as an example.
***This is the part where the stress is required.**

e.g. **A: Are yóu going to drive to the café tonight?** **B: No, Naómi will.**
1. **A: Are you going to drive to the café tonight?** **B: No, I'll walk.**
2. **A: Are you going to drive to the café tonight?** **B: No, to the store.**
3. **A: Are you going to drive to the café tonight?** **B: No, tomorrow.**

Exercise 3 Role Play

Listen to the conversation between Yoshi and Hiro from the audio. Focus on the stress, pitch and intonation and practice vocal shadowing. Then, pair up and take turns being Yoshi and Hiro to perform the conversation.

Dialogue 8

52

Yoshi: What's wrong? You look really stressed out.

Hiro: I am. My grandmother slipped and fell last night.

Yoshi: Is she OK?

Hiro: Yeah, thank goodness. She fell and banged her hip, but she didn't break anything. Anyway, the accident scared me.

Yoshi: I'll bet. Fortunately, my grandparents are still in really good shape. They all walk a lot and garden.

Hiro: My grandmother walks a lot, too. That's one reason why I'm so worried. It was the first time for me to see her as 'old.' You know what I mean?

Yoshi: I think so. So many of my memories of my grandparents are of playing outside. We used to play hide-and-seek at the park when I was a little kid. I'm not sure they'd still have the energy to do something like that now.

Hiro: Yeah. The doctor said her walking and being in good health probably saved her from a broken hip. I'm heading to her house today after classes.

Yoshi: That's a good idea. I think I'll drop by my grandparents' home this weekend.

Exercise 4 Summary

Listen to the audio and complete the summary of *Dialogue 8*.
Work with your partner and discuss your answers.

53

Hiro looks (1.) out, and Hiro reveals that her grandmother fell and got (2.) the previous night. Fortunately, Hiro's grandmother didn't (3.) any bones, but the accident made Hiro (4.) her age. During the conversation, Yoshi also (5.) his own grandparents' good health and ends by saying he will (6.) them on the weekend.

Unit 9 Reduction (2) (Final + Initial Consonant)

Tips

単語の語尾に来る子音 [p], [b], [t], [d], [k], [g] の区切りを持たずに、声門を閉じた後に直ちに後続する子音が発音される。

閉鎖音（破裂音）[p], [b], [t], [d], [k], [g] ＋子音　e.g. Stop talking.

Exercise 1

Pay attention to the reduction and read the following sentences aloud. 54

- **You should give Bob more coffee.**
- **I'll be right back.**
- **Take care of yourself.**

Exercise 2

Listen to the audio and underline the reduced parts. 55

One reason for its popularity is the energy boost we get from the caffeine in coffee.

Insects that try to eat the leaves, berries or other parts of the plant may be paralyzed or killed by the caffeine.

Exercise 3 Role Play

Listen to the conversation between Yoshi and Hiro from the audio. Focus on the reduction and practice vocal shadowing. Then, pair up and take turns being Yoshi and Hiro to perform the conversation, paying special attention to the pronunciation of the parts such as shop to, break from.

Dialogue 9

56

Yoshi: What are you doing after classes?

Hiro: I'm going to a coffee shop to study.

Yoshi: You study in a coffee shop?

Hiro: Yeah. This is a local coffee shop, not a chain. So, it's usually not crowded and the booths are comfortable.

Yoshi: I just use the library to study. It's quiet.

Hiro: I know. But I like having a cup of coffee while studying. I like the warmth and flavor. And I think the caffeine helps me to focus.

Yoshi: But doesn't it get a little bit expensive if you go there often?

Hiro: It could, but at this place you can get free refills of coffee. And like I said, it's quiet and comfortable.

Yoshi: I think I'll stick with the library. And when I need a break from studying, I go outside to a vending machine for coffee.

Exercise 4 Summary

**Listen to the audio and complete the summary of *Dialogue 9*.
Work with your partner and discuss your answers.**

57

Hiro says that she plans to study in a local café after class, which she likes because it's usually quiet and comfortable. She enjoys (1.) (2.) as it helps her focus, (3.) (4.) likes the warmth (5.) (6.). Hiro agrees it (7.) (8.) expensive, but the café offers free coffee refills. Yoshi plans to continue using the library for studying and goes outside to buy coffee from a (9.) (10.) when he needs a break.

Unit 10 Assimilation

Tips

速度の早い発話の場合は、一つの単語の最終音と後続する単語の初めの音がお互いに影響を及ぼし合い、異なる音に変化する。（同化現象）

In the case of fast pronunciation:

1. [d] + [j] ⇒ [ʤ] **Would you like to go to Antarctica?**
   [t] + [j] ⇒ [ʧ] **I've asked you the question.**
2. [z] **is she?** [izʃi(:)] ⇒ [iʃi(:)]
   [ʃ] **nice shop** [naisʃɔp] ⇒ [nə:ʃɔp] で
3. **Give me the reason why you think so.** [givmi(:)] ⇒ [gimmi(:)]
   Of course. [əvkɔ:rs] ⇒ [əfkɔ:rs]
   I have to [hævtə] ⇒ [hæftə] **go there.**

Exercise 1

Listen carefully to the audio and underline the assimilation. 58

1. Would you do me a favor?

2. Could you help me?

Exercise 2 Tongue Twister Challenge

59

Listen carefully to the audio and fill in the blank with the appropriate word. And then say the following phrase as quickly as possible three times. Start by reading the phrase slowly a few times to warm up.

(a) A runner running in the road saw a roadrunner (   ) in the road, and the roadrunner running in the road saw the runner running in the road, too. So, the (   ) and the roadrunner were running in the road together.

(b) Freshly fried (   ) French fries. Freshly fried fresh fish.

Exercise 3 Role Play

Listen to the conversation between Yoshi and Hiro from the audio. Focus on the assimilation and practice vocal shadowing. Then, pair up and take turns being Yoshi and Hiro to perform the conversation, paying special attention to the pronunciation of the parts such as "did you."

Dialogue 10

60

Yoshi: I was in science class yesterday and we talked about Antarctica. It's such a cool place.

Hiro: Is that some kind of a joke?

Yoshi: No, I mean it's an interesting place. Did you know Antarctica is the driest continent in the world and is a desert?

Hiro: Really?

Yoshi: Yeah, and it also has a blood-red waterfall.

Hiro: No way!

Yoshi: It's true. Apparently, there's this underground lake that has a lot of salt and iron in the water. When the water gets to the surface, the air rusts the iron in the water, turning it red! And get this, near the mountains there's Don Juan Pond; it's the saltiest pond on Earth, so it doesn't freeze, even at -50°C!

Hiro: Wow! I had no idea. Who's teaching this class?

Yoshi: Professor Tanaka. She's excellent! Every class is filled with interesting trivia about science. You should take it next semester. I highly recommend it.

Hiro: I'll definitely look into it.

Interesting Antarctic facts from: https://www.secretatlastravel.com/explorers-club/antarctica/50-interesting-antarctica-facts-to-inspire-your-visit/

Exercise 4 Summary

Listen to the audio and complete the summary of *Dialogue 10*.
Work with your partner and discuss your answers.

61

In a conversation about a science class, the teacher talked about interesting facts related to the (1.) of Antarctica. Antarctica is the (2.) continent in the world, and is a (3.). There is a blood-red waterfall caused by the (4.) of iron in the water. And there is also a lake called Don Juan Pond that is the saltiest lake on Earth and does not (5.), even at -50 degrees Celsius. Professor Tanaka always shares (6.) science trivia. Hiro expressed interest in the class next semester.

Reference

Reading Sections

Reading 1

Unit 2 NHK サイエンス ZERO https://www.nhk.jp/p/zero/ts/XK5VKV7V98/blog/bl/pkOaDjjMay/bp/p2peqz9pg5/

Unit 3 Retrieved on August 8, 2014 from http://edition.cnn.com/2014/05/15/travel/japan-moomin-cafe/

Unit 4 https://zatsugaku-company.com/google-name-origin/

Unit 5 https://biz-journal.jp/2023/03/post_334774.html; https://www.asahi.com/edua/article/14421975; https://www.muji.net/lab/food/201111.html

Unit 6 https://www.essentiallysports.com/us-sports-news-baseball-news-mlb-lockout-news-the-deep-reason-behind-shohei-ohtani-odd-garbage-picking-routine-on-mlb-fields-los-angeles-angels/

Unit 7 Retrieved from Wikipedia August 6, 2014 and updated from Wikipedia March 28, 2022; https://en.wikipedia.org/w/index.php?title=Harvard_University&oldid=674307319

Unit 8 Retrieved on August 17, 2014 from http://www.infiressources.ca/fer/Depotdocument_anglais/The_concept_of_humanitude_as_applied_to_general_nursing_care.pdf; Retrieved on August 13, 2014 from http://mainichi.jp/english/english/features/news/20131029p2a00m0na008000c.html

Unit 9 Retrieved on August 11, 2014 from http://blogs.scientificamerican.com/scicuriousbrain/2013/03/11/plants-give-bees-a-caffeine-buzz/

Unit 10 https://www.theworldcounts.com/populations/continents/antarctica; https://www.nasa.gov/audience/forstudents/k-4/stories/nasa-knows/what-is-antarctica-k4.html

Reading 2

Unit 1 From: https://www.thedailybeast.com/the-amazing-tale-of-paul-the-psychic-octopus-germanys-world-cup-soothsayer?ref=scroll

Unit 2 Retrieved on August 19, 2014 from http://www.space.com/22658-kirobo-talking-robot-speaksspace-video. html and http://time.com/2845040/robot-emotions-pepper-softbank/; https://www.guinnessworldrecords.com/world-records/648597-largest-robot-cheerleading-squad

Unit 3 From: https://americanhistory.si.edu/blog/mickey-mouse-turns-90

Unit 4 平成 26 年度「国語に関する世論調査」の結果の概要　文化庁 https://gogen-yurai.jp/yabai/#:~:text=%E3%82%84%E3%81%B0%E3%81%84%E3%81%AE%E8%AA%9E%E6%BA%90%E3%83%BB%E7%94%B1%E6%9D%A5,%E5%90%8C%E3%81%98%E8%AA%9E%E7%B3%BB%E3%81%A8%E8%80%83%E3%81%88%E3%82%89%E3%82%8C%E3%82%8B%E3%80%82; https://ddnavi.com/serial/722163/a/; http://www.asahi.com/special/kotoba/archive2015/danwa/2010051000016.html; https://mag.japaaan.com/archives/85862/2

Unit 6 Retrieved from Wikipedia August 5, 2014 http://www.nytimes.com/2014/02/15/sports/olympics/yuzuru-hanyu-of-japan-wins-mens-figure-skating-gold.html?_r=0; updated https://en.wikipedia.org/wiki/Yuzuru_Hanyu

Unit 7 Retrieved from Wikipedia August 6, 2014; E-journal U.S.A. 04, June, 2013

Unit 8 Retrieved on August 17, 2014 from http://www.infiressources.ca/fer/Depotdocument_anglais/The_concept_of_humanitude_as_applied_to_general_nursing_care.pdf; Retrieved on August 13, 2014 from http://mainichi.jp/english/english/features/news/20131029p2a00m0na008000c.html

Unit 9 Retrieved on August 11, 2014 from https://www.psychologytoday.com/intl/blog/brain-sense/201401/can-coffee-improve-your-memory

Listening and Speaking Sections

佐藤寧・佐藤務著『現代の音声学』金星堂

Dialogue 10 https://www.secretatlastravel.com/explorers-club/antarctica/50-interesting-antarctica-facts-to-inspire-your-visit/

Part II

Grammar Section

Unit 1　名詞の世界（1）— モノ（人、物、事）を語る

1．はじめに

名詞とは、モノ（人、物、事）を指し示す語です。「加藤さん」「あなた」「車」「水」「別れること」などが、それにあたります。「友情」「価値」「平和」といった抽象概念や、「あの日、彼女が事件現場にいたこと」といった出来事も名詞です。勿論、名詞は文の中で主役中の主役です。何しろ、「誰が」「何が」という最もスポットライトに照らされる主語や、「誰を」「何を」というもう 1 つの主役である目的語になれるのは名詞なのですから。この unit では、そんな主役を表す「名詞」について学びます。

英語の名詞表現は、日本語よりもかなり緻密《ちみつ》な規則を持っています。日本語では外来語も含めて、「家族」「紅茶」「ペット」とその名詞を覚えれば、すべてそのままの形で使えます。どんな文で使われても、「ペット」は「ペット」で OK です。しかし、英語ではそうはいかないのです。

*** I have pet.**

は、文法的に奇妙な文になってしまいます（理由は後ほど説明します）。実は、英語の名詞は文意に応じて、

I have a chicken in my room.
I had chicken for supper yesterday.
There were five chickens in his garden.
Look at the chicken over there.
All the chickens in the garden disappeared.

Tomoko has an apple for breakfast every morning.
Put some apple in the salad.
There were apples left in the box.
Give me the apple on the table.
The apples she sent me were very good.

の形が可能なのです。日本語では、すべて「鶏」「リンゴ」でコミュニケーションができることを思えば、本当に緻密です（正直、厄介《やっかい》です）。

2．an apple と apple の世界

英語では、名詞を「可算（数えられる）」か「不可算（数えられない）」かに分別して表現します。ただ、「燃えるゴミ」「燃えないゴミ」のように、その棲《す》み分けが単語ごとに決まっているのではなく、すべての名詞はどちらでも使えます。無論、人間には文化や慣習があり、言葉を使う人たちは、自分が属する文化・慣習に従ってコミュニケーションをしているので、どちらのほうで多く使われるのかという量的な違いはあります。でも、通常は「可算」だが、特別な状況では「不可算」になったり、あるいはその逆になったりと、究極、どちらにもなり得るのです。

では、可算名詞と不可算名詞を分けるものは何でしょうか？　それは具体性です。例えば、

There are five rooms in the house.
（その家には部屋が５つある）

であれば、壁や扉によって仕切られた具体的形状を持った空間、つまり、可算名詞である「部屋」ですが、

Akiko made some room for me.
（晶子さんは私のためにスペースを空けてくれた）

では、掴《つか》みどころのない不明瞭《ふめいりょう》な広がり、つまり、不可算名詞の「スペース」となります。an apple と apple の違いも同じです。

I have an apple every morning.
（毎朝リンゴを食べている）

であれば、本来の形状をしたリンゴを認知（意識）しているのに対して、

There is some grated apple in the juice.
（ジュースには摺《す》りリンゴが入っている）

では、本来の形状を失った摺り潰《つぶ》されたリンゴが認知されています。そして、この「具体性」という基準は、物理的形状だけでなく、様々なものに適用されます。

3．単数か複数か？

原則、可算名詞は単数か複数のどちらかで表現されます。これも、日本語には存在しない話し手の情報処理義務です。日本語では、名詞の複数表現は稀《まれ》です。せいぜい、「…たち」「…ら」を語尾に付け足すぐらいです。しかも、「中田くんたち」「佳子ら」など限られた名詞だけです。「冷蔵庫たち」「犬ら」とは言えません。ここでは、単数と複数に関して、特に注意すべき点を指摘しておきます。

(1) a/an と one の違い

英語を習い始めて間もない頃、「名詞が 1 つのときは、その前に a を付けます。母音の前では an になります」と教わります。そうすると、「a= 1つ」と思い込んでしまいます。実は、one → an → a と不定冠詞（a/an）が誕生する過程で（音声的にも、その流れはわかると思います）、a/an には one とは異なる働きが生まれてきました。それは、a/an には「種」を伝える機能と、「種＋数」を伝える機能があるという点です。

①「種」を伝える a/an

one にはない a/an の働きとして、「種」を伝える働きがあります。この場合、a/an は「数」を語っていません。

I like a dog.
（犬が好き）

という文を発するとき、その意識にあるのは、「他の種類の生き物」です。つまり、猫、ライオン、爬虫《はちゅう》類など他の動物との比較が潜在意識にあります。したがって、この場合、*I like one dog. と言い換えることはできません（そもそも、「1匹の犬が好き」という文は考えられません）。

②「種＋数」を伝える a/an

文意や文脈によっては、特に、動詞との関係によっては、a/an が「数」を伝えることもあります。注意して欲しいのは、その場合も、積極的に「1つ」と言っているわけではありません。だから、

I have a dog.

も「犬を飼っている」でいいのです。それが単数、つまり、「1匹」であるというのは副次的な情報です。一方、I have one dog. は、飼っている犬が「1匹」とい

う情報を積極的に伝えています。だから、one は数詞と呼ばれています。

もうおわかりですね。文は現実の場面で発せられます。どんな表現になるのかは、具体的文脈や相手との対話によって決まります。これを a/an と one について言えば、

We came here in a car.
（＜徒歩、バス、電車ではなく＞「車」で来た）→交通手段を聞かれたときの答
We came here in one car.
（「車１台」で来た）→車何台で来たのかを聞かれたときの答

となります。

(2) 複数形が意味するもの

可算名詞には複数形もあり、a/an と同じ働きがあります。即ち、「種」を伝える場合と、「種＋数」を伝える場合があるという点です。

①「種」を伝える複数形

a/an には種類を表す働きがあると説明しましたが、複数形にもそれがあります。そして、複数形は、「a/an+ 単数形」よりも可算名詞一般を語るときには多用されます。つまり、I like a dog. よりも I like dogs. のほうが広く使われています。勿論、この場合、「種」を表現しているだけなので、*I like two/a few/several/many dogs. など、数を表す語句と一緒に使うことはできません。

②「種＋数」を伝える複数形

a/an と同じく、文意や文脈によっては、複数形が「数」を伝える場合もあります。ただ、積極的に「２つ以上」と言っているわけではありません。だから、I have dogs. も、「犬を飼っている」でいいのです。それが複数であるという情報は副次的です。つまり、I have two or more dogs. と、数を強調しているのではありません。

Exercises

1 可算名詞か不可算名詞かに注意し、次の英文の（　）内に、適切な名詞を入れよ。

(1) To have a wife like her would be (　　　) on earth.
（彼女のような妻がいたら、この世の天国だろうな）

We can call this (　　　) on earth.
（ここは地上の楽園と呼べるね）

ヒント：「最高に幸せな状態」vs「幸せに生きられる場所」

(2) In order to learn about peace, you have to make a study of (　　　).
（平和について学ぶためには、戦争について研究しなければならない）

There may be (　　　) between the two countries.
（あの２国間で戦争になるかもしれない）

ヒント：「戦争（というもの）」vs「（出来事としての）戦争」

(3) This is (　　　) created by Hayato's fantasy.
（これは勇人の空想から生まれた発明品です）

Necessity is the mother of (　　　).
（必要は発明の母である）

ヒント：「発明品」vs「発明（というもの）」

(4) How many (　　　) do we have to make?
（何人分の夕食が必要ですか？）

We'll have beef for (　　　) tonight.
（今夜の夕食はビーフです）

ヒント：「（人数分の）夕食」vs「（区分を意識しない）夕食」

(5) Junko has a weakness for (　　　).
（純子はワインに目がない）

She bought us excellent (　　　) produced there.
（彼女はその地で生産されている美味しいワインを買ってくれた）

ヒント：「（液体として捉えた）ワイン」vs「（お土産に買った瓶入り）ワイン」

2 次の日本語を英訳せよ。

(1) 家族の者は、皆元気です。

ヒント：family/class/staff/team/company/audience/police/committee などの集団を表す語は、その構成員を意識するときは複数形で表す場合もある。

(2) 博はクビになりましたが（get the ax)、以前はここのスタッフでした。

ヒント：staff は、社員全体を表す集合名詞。１人の「社員」ではない。

(3) このアイスクリームの上に、スライスしたバナナを乗せてください（sliced banana)。

ヒント：スライスされたバナナの状態を考えること。

(4) ワイシャツにトマトが飛び散っているよ。

ヒント：ワイシャツに飛び散ったトマトの状態を考えること。

(5) 智子のために夕食会を開きましょう！

ヒント：「会」と言っている。

Unit 2　名詞の世界（2）― the は「情報共有」

1．はじめに

久美：　あ、スマホ、**教室**に忘れちゃった。
めぐみ：　一緒に授業を受けてた**教室**？
久美：　そう。取ってくるから、**駅**で待ってて。

日本語では、すべて「教室」「駅」で最後までコミュニケーションが可能です。でも、可算名詞と不可算名詞の区別がある英語では、一般に可算名詞として扱われる classroom, station は裸の形（何も付けない単数形）では使えないのです。では、この会話の場合は a classroom, a station で OK なのでしょうか？いえ、正解は the classroom, the station です。文脈依存性が非常に強い日本語では、話題としている名詞が何を指しているのかも文脈で判断します。上の会話で「教室」「駅」と言えば、どの教室か、どの駅かはお互い自動的に伝わります。英語ではそうはいかないのです。主語や目的語さえ省略されることの多い日本語とは違い、英語は名詞の情報共有にも標（しるし）が必要です。それが the です（例えば、日本語では、相手の目を見つめて「好き」と言えば、誰が誰を好きなのかが瞬時に伝わります。そんなとき、「誰が？」「誰を？」なんて間抜けな質問はしません。一方、英語で “Love” だけだと、「好きになれ」という命令文になってしまいます）。

では、話し手と聞き手の情報共有とはどういったことでしょうか？簡単に言えば、「どの名詞を指しているのかが聞き手にもわかる」と話し手が想定するときです。別の言い方をすれば、「話し手と聞き手の間で自動的に１つ、または、１つの集団に決まる」ということです。上の会話で the classroom, the station となるのは、どの教室、どの駅を指すのかが聞き手に特定できると話し手が思うから、つまり、２人の間では１つの教室、１つの駅に自動的に決まるからです。

2．**the** が使われる情報共有場面とは

では、どういった場面がそれに該当するのでしょうか。主として、以下の場合があります。

(1) 既に登場した名詞を指すとき

中学校で教わる the です。既に登場した名詞であれば、何を指しているのかが聞

き手にわかると話し手は思います。

I made a lot of money last month. Where has the money gone?

(2) 文脈から特定できるとき

初めて登場する名詞でも、文脈から何を指しているのかが聞き手にわかると話し手が思うときは、the が使われます。

We bought a new house. My wife loved the kitchen at first sight.

Where is the nearest bank around here?

(3) 常識から特定できるとき

「いつか月に行きたい」と言えば、「どこの月？」と確認する人はいません。常識的に、天体の月だと聞き手にわかると話し手は考えます。

Someday I want to travel to the moon.

3．その他、**the** の注意すべき点

the にはこんな使われ方もあります。

(1) 全体の中の特定領域を強調するとき

I'm surprised that he can play the violin.

楽器という全体領域の中の、「バイオリン」という特定領域です。楽器以外にも、「季節」「方角」「時間区分」「正邪」などの部分領域にも使われます。

(2) 後に置かれる説明によって、名詞が特定されるとき

なんの脈絡もなく、Akio is the man. と言えば、既にその男性が対話の中で言及されていない限り、聞き手は「え、誰のこと？」と当惑します。そこで、「明夫がその男性だよ、誰かと言えば、昨日僕が話題にした」といった補足情報があれば、the は自然な情報指定となります。

Akio is the man who(m) I talked about yesterday.

(3) その名詞に「特別感」「唯一感」「権威感」「有名感」を与えたいとき

the Bank of Japan	日本銀行
the Sea of Japan	日本海
the Amazon	アマゾン川
the Alps	アルプス
the Pacific (Ocean)	太平洋
the Sahara (Desert)	サハラ砂漠
the New York Times	ニューヨークタイムズ社
the White House	ホワイトハウス（大統領官邸）→ただの「白い家」ではありません。
the Sheraton Hotel	シェラトンホテル

などがその例です。

Exercises

1 **(1) ～ (5)** の英文 **a, b** では、同じ語に **the**（定冠詞）と **a/an**（不定冠詞）が使われているが、そのニュアンス的差異を意識しながら和訳せよ。

(1) a. I traveled around the world when I was in college.

b. It may be an unknown world for you.

(2) a. Will you exchange these dollars into Japanese yen at the bank?

b. Will you transfer the money at a bank?

(3) a. He told me the reason why he had left the company.

b. He told me a reason why he had left her.

(4) a. This is the house where Yoshiko was born.

b. This is a house where her brother grew up in his childhood.

(5) a. I have worked at a restaurant for three years. My sister began to work at the restaurant, too.

b. Megumi works part-time at a restaurant. Kumi has a part-time job at a restaurant, too.

2 次の日本語を英訳せよ。

(1) 現在には学ぶべきことが多過ぎる。

ヒント：「現在・過去・未来」（全体領域）における「現在」という特定領域への指示。

(2) 君は間違っていると思う。

ヒント：「正邪」（全体領域）における「邪」という特定領域への指示。

(3) 千春の部屋の前部は書類で覆われていた。

ヒント：**in front of** か **in the front of** か？　つまり、「部屋の扉の前」なのか、「部屋の内部空間における前の部分」なのか？

(4) トラックの前に立っているときは注意しなさい。

ヒント：前問と同様、「トラックの前」なのか、「トラックの内部空間における前の部分」なのか？

(5) ここでは左側通行をしてください。

ヒント：「左右」（全体領域）における「左」という特定領域への指示。

Unit 3　名詞の世界（3）—動詞（V）も、節（SV ...）も名詞になれる

1．はじめに

「彼女の特徴は、笑顔で不満を言うことだ（complaining/grumbling）」「母の願いは、息子が無事に就職することだった（to start his first job）」「景史郎が誠実な男だということを再認識した（that Keishiro was a sincere man）」の下線部分も、その働きは名詞です。「めぐみ」「車」「水」となんら変わりません。英語では、動詞（V）も節（SV ...）も少し形を変えるだけで、あるいは、1つ2つ単語を付け足すだけで、名詞になれるのです。ただ、文中のどこに置かれるのかが重要です。英語は、語句の配列と配置がとても重要だからです。

Humming an old tune comforts his life.
（昔の鼻歌を口ずさむことが、彼に安らぎを与えている）

The man humming an old tune is my father.
（昔の鼻歌を口ずさんでいる男性が、私の父です）

He was walking in the park, humming an old tune.
（昔の鼻歌を口ずさみながら、彼は公園を歩いていた）

1文目は名詞、2文目は形容詞、3文目は副詞の働きをしています。日本語は少しずつ語尾を変化させて働きを変えますが、英語はまったく同じです。すべて、humming an old tune です。ただ、どこに置くかによって、文中での働きも違ってくるのです。この unit では、人や物以外でも、名詞の働きができる仲間を紹介します。

2．動詞（V）を少し弄《いじ》ると、名詞になれる

(1) ing

動詞に ing を付けただけで、「…すること」という名詞になれます。「…する」という動詞的な要素を含んでいながら、最終的には「こと」という名詞の働きをするので、「動名詞」と呼ばれています。この名詞の特徴は、ing（…している）という形からわかるように、静止画像ではなく、動画のイメージです。「動いている」映像を想像してください。勿論、文中では、名詞の働きをする場所に置かなければなりません。

Driving with my wife was great fun.

（妻とのドライブは、本当に楽しかった）

Hiroshi likes drinking with Junichi.

（博は準一と一杯やるのが好きだ）

I look forward to visiting Masafumi's office.

（正史のオフィスを訪ねることを楽しみにしています）

(2) to V

「to+ 動詞の原形」として教わる「to 不定詞」です。２語で one set と考えましょう。to 不定詞の起源は、「行為（すること）」を表す目的で、動詞が文中で主語や目的語として用いられたことにあります。やがて、古英語から中期英語の時代に入ると、最初は主語の位置で to V 型となり、やがて目的語の位置でも to V 型となっていきます。つまり、to 不定詞は、「名詞用法（すること）」から始まりました。もちろん、今の英語でも、その形で使われています。

To say such a shabby thing was the last thing she thought of.

（そんな卑しい発言をすることは、彼女には思いもよらなかった）

My dream is to become a judo medalist in the Olympic Games.

（僕の夢は、オリンピックの柔道でメダリストになることだ）

さて、to と言えば、既にお気付きだと思います。そう、前置詞にも to がありますね。例えば、Yoshiko went to Hotel Okura in Kobe の to です。実は、to 不定詞の to も、その起源は前置詞です。前置詞 to のイメージは、「…へ向かう」「…へ到達する」「…と結び付く」です。したがって、to 不定詞には元来、「進む方向＝未来」が含まれていました。

Yoshiko decided to visit her ex-boyfriend.

（佳子は元彼を訪ねることに決めた）

佳子が visit するのは、述語動詞（decided）よりも後で起きます。hope, want, desire, expect, require, decide, promise, agree, refuse など、願望、欲求、期待、要求、決断、約束、同意、拒絶等を表す動詞の目的語の位置に、「後で起きる」ことを意味する to 不定詞が置かれるのはそのためです。また、動名詞と違って、to

不定詞には動画のような躍動感はありません。静止画像、言い換えれば、「(例えば)…することは」といった一般論や、「…するようなことになれば」といった仮定を表します。

(3) 節（SV ...）

節とは、文（SV ...）を構成する一部ですが、それ自体がSとVを持っています。ただ、その前に節を作るための語句（接続詞や疑問詞）が必要です。そして、節全体が名詞の働きをするものを「名詞節」と呼んでいます。具体的に見ていきましょう。先ずは、代表格のthatです。

That Takafumi had respect for Akio was surprising to Masafumi.

（貴文が明夫に敬意を抱いていることは、正史とって意外だった）

Takafumi had respect for Akioで文が成立しているのに、その直後にwas surprising to Masafumiと文らしきものが続くと、聞き手は、「どうなっているの？」と当惑してしまいます。そこで、「ここまでの部分は名詞だよ」と教えてくれる標識が必要になります。その標識の代表格がthatです。thatと聞けば、「それ」を思い出すでしょう。実は、「それ」のthatと本質的には同じです。同じ単語なのですから。次のように考えてください。

Atsuko said that she was going to set out on an aimless journey.
S V O

（敦子は、放浪の旅に出るつもりだと言った）

最初に、「敦子は言った」と主語・動詞（SV）がきて、「言った」の目的語として、「それはね（that）... ということを」となります。つまり、「それは」と対象を指示するthatと同じです。「それはね」という感覚で捉えてください。

名詞節を作れるのはthatだけではありません。疑問詞（who, what, when, where, why, how, etc.）もOKです。「夫が何をしでかしたか（ということ　what her husband did)」「博が年間いくら稼いでいるのか（ということ　how much Hiroshi earns per year)」「どうして、明夫がそんなに早く帰宅するのか（ということ　why Akio leaves the office so early)」という日本語からもわかると思います。

Exercises

1 次の（　　）内の語句を並べ替えて、日本語に合う適切な英文を作れ。尚、文頭に置かれる語も小文字で記している。

(1) [constant, me, her, to, irritating, she, nagging, is] ＜1語不要＞

（彼女がいつもガミガミ言うのにはウンザリだ）

ヒント：**ing** は名詞の働きができる。そして、その **ing** を誰がするのかを表したいときは、**ing** の前にそれを置く必要がある。これを「動名詞の意味上の主語」と言う。

(2) [showing, know, necessary, not, any sign, knowing, is, of] ＜1語不要＞

（知っている素振りを見せないことが必要だ）

ヒント：・否定詞（**not, never**）は、**ing** の前に置く。
・前置詞の目的語には、原形不定詞（動詞の原形）は使わない。

(3) [is, rub, good, the wrong way, me, at, he, rubbing, to] ＜2語不要＞

（あの人の特技は、私の神経を逆撫でするることです）

ヒント：前置詞の目的語に **to V** は置けない。この **to** も元々は前置詞なので、前置詞が2つ続くことになってしまうため（日本語で、「私はを」がダメなのと同じ感覚）。

(4) [anything, to, be wise, it, say, at the meeting, not, will] ＜すべて使用＞

（会議では、何も言わないことが賢明だろう）

ヒント：・形式主語構文。英語では、新しい情報や情報量の多い部分は、頭でっかちな文構造を避けるために、後ろに置かれる傾向がある（「文末焦点の原則」「文末重点の原則」）。これは、聞き手の心理的負担を軽減し、聞き逃しのリスクを少なくするための機能的な文法規則である。形式主語構文もそうした目的で使われる。「本当の主語は後に登場しますが、『それ』ということにしておきましょう」といった感覚。
・否定詞は **to V** の前に置く。

(5) [with, idea, Kunio, out, had, to, Tess, no, where, go] <すべて使用>

（テスとどこでデートしたらいいのか、邦男にはわからなかった）

ヒント：「疑問詞（**what, when, where, which, how etc.**）＋ **to V**」も、名詞の働きができる。その際、「…すべき」という義務的ニュアンスが強い（例：**when to start**　いつ始めるべきか）。

2 次の日本語を英訳せよ。

(1) 光司が明日来るかどうかは、重要ではない。

ヒント：「二択」を表す疑問詞がヘッドになる名詞 **chunk**（塊）を作る。

(2) あの常連客（regular customer）は、陽子がどこに住んでいるのかを知りたがっている。

ヒント：「場所」を表す疑問詞がヘッドになる名詞 **chunk** を作る。

(3) あいつらとは二度と口を聞かないと、博は怒って言った。

ヒント：**that** がヘッドになる名詞 **chunk** を作る。

(4) あの先生は理路整然と話すことができないので、会議で何を言おうとしていたのかは、誰にもわからなかった。

ヒント：「何を」を表す疑問詞がヘッドになる名詞 **chunk** を作る。

(5) 夫が今まで何回自動車事故を起こしたのか、想像できないと思いますよ。

ヒント：・**that** がヘッドになる名詞 **chunk** を作る。
・「回数」を表す疑問詞がヘッドになる名詞 **chunk** を作る。

Unit 4　修飾の世界（1）— 名詞を前から修飾すれば「限定」

1．はじめに

名詞を飾る（修飾する）品詞は「形容詞」と言われています。これは、英語でも同じです。warmhearted person（優しい人）、beautiful flowers（綺麗な花）のwarmhearted/beautifulは、名詞person/flowersを修飾する形容詞の働きをしています。では、修飾とは、どういった意味なのでしょうか？それは、性質や状態を述べることによって、「名詞を限定している」＝「名詞の範囲を絞っている」ということです。「優しい人」と「人」のどちらの集合が大きいのかは自明の理です。前者の集合は、後者の集合に包含されます。「人」の中には、「ケチな人」「勇敢な人」「酒乱の人」など、様々な部分集合が存在します。「優しい人」も、「人」という全体集合を限られた範囲に絞っています。「美味しいコーヒー」「背が高い女性」が、コーヒーや女性の範囲を絞っているのも同様です。このように、英語では、形容詞が前から名詞を修飾する場合は（これを「前置修飾」と言います）、その名詞の範囲を限定している（絞っている）と考えてください。

2．修飾には順番がある

形容詞には、「優しい」「魅力的な」「面白い」といった主観的・評価的内容を表すものもあれば、「新しい」「木製の」「日本の」といった客観的・記述的内容を表すものもあります。日本語では、「背の高いアメリカの若くて魅力的な女性」と言っても、「若いアメリカの魅力的で背の高い女性」と言っても、あまり気になりません。英語でも、絶対的なルールがあるわけではありませんが、一般的に、複数の形容詞を並べて修飾するときは、その順番に次のような傾向があります。

①「**主観的・評価的**」→ ②「**記述的・知覚的**」→ ③「**属性的・素材的**」

この傾向に沿って、上記日本語を英訳すれば、

an attractive, tall, young, American woman

となります。ただ、同じグループ内での順番は厳密ではありません。記述的・知覚的グループ内のtallとyoungは交換可能です。

３．形が変わると形容詞

(1) ing

置かれる場所によって、ing が名詞（動名詞）になることは説明しました。同じ ing であっても、名詞を前から修飾する場所に置かれると、形容詞になります。これを現在分詞と言います。進行形で使われる ing と同じです。「笑っている赤ちゃん」「走っている馬」は、smiling baby/galloping horse となります。但し、「…している」となるのは、「笑う」「走る」「流れる」などの自動詞の場合です。他動詞の ing は、「…させる」という意味になります。例えば、excite（興奮させる）の場合、exciting games になれば、「（人を）興奮させる試合」→「面白い試合」となります。

(2) 過去分詞

過去分詞も形容詞の仲間です。名詞の前に置かれると、直接その名詞を修飾します。broken heart（「壊された心」→「失意、失恋」）のように、過去分詞は、「された / される」といった受け身の意味になります。このとき、surprise（驚かす）、excite（興奮させる）、disappoint（がっかりさせる）、delight（喜ばせる）などの感情を表す他動詞の場合、注意すべき点があります。日本語では「驚いた観客」であっても、観客は驚かされているので、英語では surprised spectators と表現します。反対に、「驚くべき知らせ」は、news が人を驚かす内容なので、surprising news となります。

尚、自動詞（帰る、辞める、流れる、落ちる等）の場合は、retired people（辞めた人→退職者）、fallen leaves（落ちた葉→落ち葉）のように、「…した」という完了の意味になります。

(3) 複合名詞（名詞 ＋ 名詞 ＝ 新しい名詞）

日本語でも名詞を連続させて、１つの新しい名詞を生み出すことができますね。「消費者＋団体＝消費者団体」「日本＋空手道＋連盟＝日本空手道連盟」といったように。英語も同じです。名詞を連結させて、新しい名詞を作ることができます。そうした名詞を「複合名詞」と言います。このとき、前に置かれた名詞は、形はそのままでも、後ろの名詞を修飾する形容詞の働きをします。school bus（学バス）がその一例で、school 自体は名詞ですが、後ろの bus を修飾する形容詞として機能しています。なぜ、名詞を並べる必要があるのかと言えば、schooling bus だと、「教育用バス」「研修用バス」といった意味になってしまうからです。昔、人気を博したアニメ？ DEATH NOTE も、名詞 DEATH（死）が名詞 NOTE を修飾する形容詞の働きをしています。形容詞 DEAD だと、DEAD NOTE（死んだメモ）となり、まったく怖くないからです。

Exercises

1 形容詞の中には「数量形容詞」と呼ばれ、「数」や「量」を表すものがあり、「すべての」「ほとんどの」「多くの」「いくつかの」「漠然とした」「少しの」「ほとんどない」「まったくない」「それぞれの」「両方の」「どちらかの」など、多岐にわたっている。日本語を参考にして、下記の（ ）内に適切な数量形容詞を入れよ。

(1) (　　　　　) member of the club has a right to use the facilities.

（クラブのすべての会員には、施設を利用できる権利がある）

ヒント：「（**A** くん、**B** くん、**C** くん、**D** くん…まとめて）すべて」**or**「（**A** くんも、**B** くんも、**C** くんも、**D** くんも…それぞれ）すべて」？つまり、全体に焦点あるのか、個々に焦点があるのか？ 動詞 **has** がヒント。

(2) (　　　　) one of you needs to have enough self-awareness as a member of society.

（君たちは各自、社会の一員としての自覚を持たなければならない）

ヒント：全体への意識が **every** よりも更に薄くなり、個々への意識がより強い語。まさに、「各々の」「それぞれの」といった感覚。

(3) (　　　　　) people here are growing disgusted with her one-sided argument.

（彼女の一方的な言い分に、反感を持ち始めている人もいる）

ヒント：「漠然とした」「ぼんやりとした」感覚。単数にも複数にも使えるが、具体的にはわからない、言えない、言いたくないときの感覚。決して、「いくつか」といった数を意識したニュアンスではない。

(4) I didn't see (　　　　) professors at university today.

（今日、大学ではどの教授にも会わなかった）

ヒント：「どんな…でも」といった選択の任意性を表す語。学校では、否定文と疑問文で使われると教わるが、「どの…を選んでも」といった感覚で、肯定文でも使える。

(5) Be careful! (　　　　) pets are allowed here.

（注意してください。ここはペット禁止です）

ヒント：「０×名詞＝０」と考える。「まったく…ない」という強烈な否定イメージ。

(6) Keishiro has visited Shanghai (　　　　) times to see her.

（彼女と会うため、景史郎は上海を数回訪れたことがある）

ヒント：「いくつか」と言いたいときは、**some** ではなく、この語を用いる。

(7) There are not so (　　　　) kinds of animals in the zoo.

（あの動物園には、それほど多くの種類の動物はいない）

ヒント：可算名詞に用いられる「多くの」は？

(8) Why did that woman drink so (　　　　) sake last night?

（昨夜、あの女性はそんなに酒を飲んだのですか？）

ヒント：不可算名詞に用いられる「多くの」は？

(9) I couldn't understand (　　　　) sentences of the report because it was written in Japanese.

（日本語で書かれていたため、報告書のほとんどの文を理解できなかった）

ヒント：可算名詞にも不可算名詞にも使える「ほとんどの」は？

(10) My husband has had (　　　　) friends to talk to in his life.

（夫には、今まで相談できる友人がほとんどいなかった）

ヒント：可算名詞に用いられる「ほとんどない」は？

(11) There was (　　　　　) beer left after those women went out.

（あの女性たちが出て行った後は、ビールはほとんど残っていなかった）

ヒント：不可算名詞に用いられる「ほとんどない」は？

(12) (　　　　　) the students should be treated equal here.

（ここでは、すべての学生が平等に扱われるべきである）

ヒント：全部ひっくるめて「すべての」は？

(13) Drive your car with (　　　　　) hands!

（両手で運転しろ！）

ヒント：対象が2つあり、「両方の」は？

(14) (　　　　　) car will be OK as long as one gets started.

（エンジンがかかるなら、どっちの車でもいいよ）

ヒント：対象が2つあり、「どちらでも」は？

(15) Keishiro thought that he would see (　　　) woman anymore.

（景史郎は、どちらの女性にも二度と会うことはないだろうと思った）

ヒント：対象が2つあり、「どちらも…ない」は？

2 (　) 内の語を使って、次の日本語を英訳せよ。書き出しの英語が与えられているものもある。

(1) 昨日、敦は社長から驚くべき知らせを受け取った (surprise)。

____

ヒント：**surprise** は「…を驚かせる」という意味の他動詞。

(2) 正史の同僚が目にしたのは、彼の度肝を抜く酒量だった (petrify)。

What Masafumi's colleagues saw was ____________________

____

ヒント：**petrify** は「…を固める」「…の度肝を抜く」という意味の他動詞。

(3) イライラした表情が小百合の顔に浮かんだのは、母親があのブラジルの歌を歌ったときだった (irritate)。

____

____

ヒント：**irritate** は「…をイライラさせる」という意味の他動詞。

Unit 5　修飾の世界（2）— 名詞の後ろに置けば「追加情報」

1．はじめに

日本語では、「自宅の庭で枯れてしまった花」「神戸に住んでいる彼の恋人」「昨年、旅先の函館で出合った女の子」など、名詞を修飾する表現は、短くても長くても前に置かれます。しかし、英語には、flowers withered in my garden, his partner living in Kobe, the girl who I met in Hakodate while traveling last year と、後ろから修飾する仕組みがあります。この修飾は、「後置修飾」と呼ばれています。
では、前置修飾との一番の違いは何でしょうか？　前回の unit で、「前からの修飾は、性質や状態を述べることによって名詞を限定している＝名詞の範囲を絞っている」と述べました。これに対して、後ろからの修飾は「追加情報」、つまり、前の名詞がどんな名詞なのかを追加説明している感覚だと捉えてください。例えば、You need a flexible thought.（君には柔軟な思考が必要だ）では、flexible は thought に備わった属性を表していますが、You need a thought flexible enough to adapt to those changes.（君には、そうした変化に適応できる柔軟な思考が必要だ）では、相手に思考が必要だと述べて後で、その思考がどういった内容なのかを説明しています。この unit では、そうした後置修飾の方法を紹介します。

2．後置修飾の方法

後置修飾には、いくつかの方法があります。代表的なパターンは、「形容詞を含んだ chunk（塊）」「前置詞＋名詞」「現在分詞 / 過去分詞」「関係詞節」です。順番に見ていきましょう。

(1) 形容詞を含んだ chunk

She sent me a box full of big pears.
（彼女は大きな梨でいっぱいの箱を送ってくれた）

どんな箱なのかを、full of big pears が追加情報として説明しています。

(2) 前置詞＋名詞

「前置詞＋名詞」は、後置修飾の中で最もよく使われます。特に、空間・位置、状態、所有を表す場合に多用されます。

Look at that luxury car in the garage!
（ガレージの中のあの高級車を見てみろよ！）

The number of people with the disease has been increasing three times every two months.
（罹患者の数は、２ヵ月毎に３倍の速度で増えている）

in the garage が car を、of people が number を、with the disease が people を修飾しています。「高級車がどこにあるのか」「なんの数なのか」「どんな人なのか」を、「前置詞＋名詞」が追加情報として説明しています。

(3) 現在分詞 / 過去分詞

現在分詞（ing）も過去分詞も、名詞を後ろから修飾できます。

The woman standing by me turned around when she saw policemen.
（私の側に立っていた女性は、警官を見たとき向きを変えた）

Please have a look on your right. Mt. Fuji covered with snow looks beautiful from the window.
（右手をご覧ください。窓から雪で覆われた富士山が綺麗に見えます）

「女性が何をしていたのか」「どんな富士山なのか」を、分詞が追加情報として説明しています。

(4) 関係詞節

日本語では、「昨年のクーデータ以来、内乱、暴動、抑圧、虐殺などが頻発している政情不安定な国」といったように、修飾部分がどんなに長くても、前から名詞を修飾します。一方、英語では名詞を修飾する節（SV…）は、必ず後ろから説明を加えます。この代表例が関係詞（関係代名詞、関係副詞）です。

Who's Hiroshi?
（博って、誰？）

He is the man who Tomoharu and Junichi always make fun of.

（智治と準一がいつもからかっている男だよ）

I want to visit that place again where I met Shizuka ten years ago.

（１０年前に静と出会ったあの場所へもう一度行きたい）

「博とは男だよ。誰か（who）って言えば、智治と準一がいつもからかっている」「あの場所へもう一度行きたい。どこか（where）って言えば、静と 10 年前に出会った場所さ」といったように、関係詞節が追加情報として man や place を説明しています。

Exercises

1 次の（　　）内の語句を並べ替えて、日本語に合う適切な英文を作れ。尚、文頭に置かれる語も小文字で記している。

(1) [for, anger, Mr. Nojima, his school days, Mr. Sakakibara, of, remembered, as being full]

（榊原氏は、野島氏への怒りでいっぱいの学生時代を思い出した）

ヒント：「どんな学生時代だったのか」を説明する形容詞句。

(2) [Chiharu's desk, at, documents, look, on, the pile of]

（千春の机の上に積み上げられた書類を見てごらん）

ヒント：「書類の山がどこにあるのか」を説明する「前置詞＋名詞」

(3) [that bench, Junko, on, is, eating ice cream, the woman]

（あそこのベンチでアイスクリームを食べている女性が純子です）

ヒント：「女性が何をしているのか」を説明する現在分詞。

(4) [along, loved, with, my wife, the streets, Christmas lights, walking, decorated]

（妻は、クリスマスのイルミネーションに彩られた通りを歩くのが好きだった）

ヒント：「どんな通りなのか」を説明する過去分詞。

(5) [beautiful, was, my wife, up, the town, looked, where, brought]

（妻が生まれ育った町は美しかった）

ヒント：「どんな町なのか」を説明する関係副詞節。

2 （　）内の語を使って、次の日本語を英訳せよ。書き出しの英語が与えられているものもある。

(1) まだデザートは入りますか？（room）

＿＿＿＿＿＿＿＿＿＿＿＿＿＿＿＿＿＿＿＿＿＿＿＿＿＿＿＿＿＿

ヒント：この **room** は「余地」という意味。つまり、「デザートが食べられる余地が（お腹に）ありますか？」という意味。

(2) 博史の長話にウンザリした参加者たちは、二度とここへは来ないと決めた（sick and tired of, long talk）。

The participants ＿＿＿＿＿＿＿＿＿＿＿＿＿＿＿＿＿＿＿＿＿＿＿＿

＿＿＿＿＿＿＿＿＿＿＿＿＿＿＿＿＿＿＿＿＿＿＿＿＿＿＿＿＿＿

ヒント：「参加者がどういった状態だったのか」を説明する。

(3) あいつは、三宮駅のホームで彼らをボコボコに殴った理由を覚えていない（beat ... to a pulp）。

＿＿＿＿＿＿＿＿＿＿＿＿＿＿＿＿＿＿＿＿＿＿＿＿＿＿＿＿＿＿

ヒント：「どんな理由なのか」を説明する関係副詞節。

(4) 佳子は、国税局査察官の兄を持つクラスメートです（a national tax investigator）。

＿＿＿＿＿＿＿＿＿＿＿＿＿＿＿＿＿＿＿＿＿＿＿＿＿＿＿＿＿＿

ヒント：「どんなクラスメート」なのかを説明する関係代名詞節。

(5) 私が 5 年以上付き合った男は、二股野郎だった（go out with, a two-timing lowlife）。

＿＿＿＿＿＿＿＿＿＿＿＿＿＿＿＿＿＿＿＿＿＿＿＿＿＿＿＿＿＿

ヒント：「どんな男なのか」を説明する関係代名詞節。

Unit 6　動詞の世界（1）―文の型を決めるのは動詞！働きかけの対象がない自動詞と、それが必要な他動詞

1．はじめに

「水が流れる」「鳥は飛ぶ」といった文は、短いながらも、完成しています。それは、「流れる」「飛ぶ」は、「…を」という対象（目的語）を必要としないからです。「博は衰えた」「火事が起きた」「彼女は眠った」なども同様です。このように、「…を」「…に」といった対象を取らない動詞を「自動詞」と言います。高校の授業で学習する、

第１文型：	**SV**	**V**＝自動詞
第２文型：	**SVC**	**V**＝自動詞
第３文型：	**SVO**	**V**＝他動詞
第４文型：	**SVOO**	**V**＝他動詞
第５文型：	**SVOC**	**V**＝他動詞

という基本５文型中の第１文型と第２文型で使われる動詞です。これに対して、対象であるＯ（目的語）を必要とする第３～５文型の動詞は、「他動詞」と呼ばれています。主語が他者へ作用や影響を与えるからです。ただ、多くの動詞は、自動詞用法と他動詞用法の両方を持っています（歴史的にどちらの用法から始まったのか、また、現在はどちらで使われることが多いのかという違いはありますが）。このunitでは、先ず、同じ基本動詞が自動詞としても、他動詞としても使われることを学びます。次に、他動詞の場合、主語が他者から作用を受けることもあります（「みんな彼女を好き→彼女はみんなに好かれている」）。それを「受動態」と呼びますが、そのポイントを簡単にお伝えします。

2．動詞の作用が直接加わるとは ― 自動詞と他動詞

次の英文を見てください。

a. A stranger attacked.
b. A stranger attacked me.

「見知らぬ人が襲ってきた」というaの文では、攻撃対象を述べていないため、attackedは自動詞として使われています。それに対して、bでは、attackedの作用が直接meに及んでいます。まさに、見知らぬ人から直接攻撃を受けたことを意味

しています。以下の例文も同様です。

c. Atsuko heard the sound last night.
S　V　O
（昨夜、敦子は例の物音を聞いた）

d. Atsuko heard about Keishiro last night.
S　V
（昨夜、敦子は景史郎のことを聞いた）

e. Atsuko heard of Keishiro last night.
S　V
（昨夜、敦子は景史郎のことを耳にした）

c では、聴覚作用が物音に直接及んでいます。つまり、物音を直接聞いたのです。一方、前置詞 about が入っている d では、heard の作用が景史郎に直接及んでいません。つまり、敦子が景史郎の音声（言葉）を直接聞いたのではなく、景史郎に関する情報を聞いたという意味です。例えば、景史郎は誠実な人だとか、優しい男だとか、常識人だとかいった情報を誰かから聞いたというニュアンスです。更に、e の前置詞 of になると、「耳にした程度」といった意味合いが強くなります。

だから、I miss you. と言ってこそ、相手に思いが伝わり、また、Shinko kicked Masafumi when he was down.（真子は正史の弱みにつけ込んで酷いことをした）と言ってこそ、正史が酷い行為を受けたことが伝わります。

3．受動態とは ― 主語が作用を受ける

態には、「能動態」と「受動態」の２つがあります。能動態とは主語が他者に作用を与える、受動態とは主語が他者から作用を受けるということです。例えば、

Hiroshi hit Junichi.
（博が準一を蹴った）

では、博が準一に蹴りという作用を与えています。一方、

Junichi was hit by Hiroshi.
（準一は博に蹴られた）

では、準一は博から蹴りという作用を受けています。物であれ、感情であれ、このように主語が他者から何かを受ける（される）表現を受動態と言います。

(1) 受動態が必要なとき

受動態は「be 動詞＋過去分詞」という形で作ります。それでは、どんな場合に受動態が使われるのでしょうか。大きく分けると、次の 4 つが考えられます

① 前文の話題を、次の文の主語で引き継ぐとき

日本語でも、「景史郎ってどんな人？」「勇敢だから、みんなに尊敬されているよ」といった類の会話はよくあります。英語も同じです。topicalization（話題化）と呼ばれ、会話の自然な流れから、テーマを文頭に移動させて話題を引き継ぐ手法が取られることがあります。そうした際、倒置形（例：SVO → OSV）や受動態が使われます。

What is Keishiro like?
（景史郎ってどんな人？）

—Oh, he is respected by everyone here because he is so brave.
（勇敢だから、みんなに尊敬されているよ）

② 情報量が多い部分や新情報を文末に置くとき

英語には「文末重点の原則」（principle of end-weight）や「文末焦点の原則」（principle of end-focus）があり、情報量の多い部分や新情報は文末に置かれる傾向があります。それらを文頭に置くと、記憶や情報処理に手間を要し、また、聞き逃しのリスクや心理的負担が高まるからです。

Shizuka was shocked by the fact that Keishiro had decided to leave Shanghai.
（景史郎が上海を去る決心をしたという事実に、静はショックを受けた）

③ 誰がするのかを言う必要がないとき

「オーストラリアの人々は、オーストラリアでは英語を話している」と言う必要はありません。

English is spoken in Australia.
（オーストラリアでは英語が話されている）

④ 文に客観的な印象を持たせたいとき

日本語ではあまり意識されませんが、英語では、「無生物→動物→人間」と親近感が強くなっていきます。したがって、客観的な印象を与えなければならない論文や報告書では、親近感、言い換えれば、主観的な響きを排除するために無生物を主語に置く文体が多く取られます。

It is said that too much pacifism will put us in danger of causing aggression.
（行き過ぎた平和主義が、侵略を誘発する危険性があると言われている）

(2) どんな文でも受動態にできるわけではない

中学校で受動態を習ったとき、能動態の目的語（例：SVO の O）を主語にすれば、自動的に受動態が作れると思った人もいるかもしれませんが、どんな文でも機械的に受動態にできるわけではありません。受動態が使われるためには、主語（作用を受けるもの）が、動作主（by ～で表されるもの）の行為によって何らかの影響を受けなければなりません。例えば、

***The town was reached by me yesterday.**
（昨日、町は私によって到達された）

という文は不適格です。町は個人の到達を受けても、何ら影響を受けないからです。一方、

The town was attacked by terrorists yesterday.
（町は昨日テロリストの襲撃を受けた）

は適格な文です。テロリストの襲撃を受けると、住民が殺傷されたり、物が破壊されたりと、町は影響を受けるからです。

(3) 受動態では絶対に by を使うの？

「…によって」の部分には、前置詞 by を用います。by の本質は「側（そば）」ですが、行為は、通常、側にいる者によって行われるからです。でも、at, with, of などの

前置詞が使われることもあります。これは、その動詞と前置詞が持つイメージに理由があります。例えば、

Mr. Yasuda was surprised/excited at the news of Mr. Saito's marriage.
（安田さんは、斎藤さんの結婚に驚いた / 興奮した）

Mr. and Mrs. Saito were satisfied/delighted with many congratulations from their colleagues.
（斎藤さん夫妻は、同僚たちからの祝福に満足していた / 喜んでいた）

This car is made of plastic.
（この車はプラスティックでできている）

という文では、at, with, of といった前置詞が使われています。これは、「驚き」「興奮」は瞬間的な感情なので（３日間同じことで驚き続けている人はいません）、「地点」を表す at が、「満足」「喜び」はジワーっとした比較的持続性のある感情なので、「共に」を表す with がイメージに合致するからです。また、「…から作られている」では、原材料を述べているので、「母集団」を本質とする of が使われています。学校ではこれらを特別な受動態として覚えさせられますが、何ら特別ではありません。

Exercises

1 動詞の右側の構造に注意しながら、それぞれの英文を和訳せよ。

(1) a. He left without saying goodbye.

b. My husband left us nothing.

ヒント：・a の **left** には目的語がない。**without** は、「…なしで /…しないで」という意味の前置詞。
・b の **left** には目的語がある。

(2) a. We have been making fun of Hiroshi since our high school days.

b. My wife always makes me fantastic meals.

c. That remark made her blog swarm with negative comments.

ヒント：・a の **make fun of** は成句だが、分析的に言えば、**fun** が **make** の目的語であり、前置詞 **of** は「材料」を表している。つまり、「**Hiroshi** を材料にして **fun** を作ってきた」という意味。
・b では、**made** の目的語は **me** と **meals** の２つ。
・c は、「**remark** が、**blog** = **swarm** になる状況を作った」という意味。**swarm with ...**　…が群がっている→ネットでは「炎上」に近い。

(3) a. Kaoru in my memory keeps smiling.

b. The news of the class reunion couldn't keep Tomoharu from laughing.

c. Keishiro is a sincere man and always keeps his word.

d. Those remarks made me hit the ceiling.

ヒント：・a は、「**Kaoru** = **smiling** の状況が続いている」という意味。
・b と c の **keep(s)** には目的語がある。
・d は、「**me** が **hit the ceiling** する状況を作った」という意味。

2 次の（　　）内から正しいものを選べ。

(1) Don't talk to Junko now. Her pudding went (bad, badly) and she is so upset.

ヒント：**go, come, get, turn, run, fall, grow** などの「移動」を表す動詞は、「ある状態が別の状態への移動する」という意味から、「**S** は **C** へ状態変化する（**S** は **C** になる）」を表すことができる。但し、同じ「…になる」であっても、その動詞が持つ基本イメージの影響を受けている。

(2) Things will come out (all right, all rightly).

ヒント：話し手から離れていくイメージの **go** に対して、**come** は話し手の領域へやって来るイメージ。どちらのイメージがいいのかは、自明の理。

(3) I sent the materials (to, in, of) Akio, a psychologist.

ヒント：前置詞 **to** は「方向」、**in** は「３次元的空間」、**of** は「母集団」と考えるとわかり易い。では、**send**（送る）と相性がいいのは？

(4) Will you get some bottles of wine (about, for, of) the party?

ヒント：「受益者」のイメージを持つ前置詞は？

(5) Masafumi asked (to, for, of) Chiharu what had happened

ヒント：英語には「文末重点の原則」「文末焦点の原則」があり、情報量の多い部分や、新情報は文末に置かれる傾向がある。ここでは、**asked** の目的語 **what had happened** が文末に置かれている。では、情報の出所に馴染む前置詞は？

(6) Unfortunately, my ex-girlfriend (married, married with) a wealthy oddball.

ヒント：「結婚する」は、神父さんや牧師さんに式を挙げてもらっていたので、受身（**be married**）で表現されることもあるが、「僕と結婚してください」というプロポーズの言葉は他動詞として使われる（**Will you marry me?**）。他動詞には前置詞は必要か？　**I love you** を考えれば、答は明白。

(7) Tomoharu looks happy when he (describes, describes about) the incidents about Hiroshi.

ヒント：**discuss**（…について議論する）、**describe**（…について述べる）、**mention**（…について言及する）などの動詞は、「…について」という日本語から、前置詞 **about** が必要に思えるが、目的語である話題やテーマに直接言い及ぶイメージが強いので、他動詞として使われる。

3 受動態が使われるためには、主語が動作主（**by ...**）の行為によって、何らかの影響を受けなければならないとされている。次の２つの英文のうち、受動態としてより適格なものを選べ。

(1) a. Tokyo will have to be reached by me.

b. The agreement must be reached among them.

ヒント：東京は個人の到達を受けて影響を受けるのか？

(2) a. This bed was slept in by the suspect last night.

b. This bed was slept in by my younger sister last night.

ヒント：使用されたことによって、ベッドに証拠価値を与えたのは？

(3) a. Our university will be visited by some neighbors next week.

b. Our university will be visited by the U.S. President next week.

ヒント：訪問することによって、大学の名声に影響を与えるのは？

(4) a. Mt. Fuji was climbed by so many people last year.

b. Mt. Fuji was climbed by my mother last year.

ヒント：登山によって、環境・衛生・景観などの面で富士山に影響を与えるのは？

4 次の英文を受動態に書き換えよ。

(1) They speak French in that country.

____

ヒント：・**speak** の目的語 **French** を主語にする。
・**by them** は不要。「その国の人たちによって」は自明の理。

(2) Someone broke the window.

____

ヒント：・**broke** の目的語 **window** を主語にする。

(3) Hiroshi laughed at Tomoharu, who had thought the graduation ceremony would be in the afternoon.

ヒント：・**(laughed) at** の目的語 **Tomoharu** を主語にする。
・**graduation ceremony**　卒業式

(4) People say that the psychologist is a henpecked husband.

ヒント：・**say** の目的語 **that ... husband**（名詞節）を主語にする。通例、こうした場合、仮主語 **it** が用いられる。
・**by people** は不要。「世間の人によって」は自明の理。
・**henpecked husband**　恐妻家

(5) That female professor has hurt the assistants for a long time.

ヒント：・**has hurt** の目的語 **assistants** を主語にする。
・現在完了形の受動態。
・**hurt** は不規則変化。

(6) They will elect Masafumi (the) president of the university.

ヒント：・**elect** の目的語 **Masafumi** を主語にする。
・助動詞を含んだ受動態。
・**They** が誰を指すのかが明白な場合、**by them** は不要。

Unit 7　動詞の世界（2）—「過去と未来」を語る仕組み

1．はじめに

文法の授業で、「時制」という言葉をよく耳にすると思います。時制とは、伝えようとしている事柄（出来事）がいつ起きたのかを、動詞によって表したものです。事柄には始まりと終わりがあり、現在よりも前に起きたのか、後に起きるのかを伝える必要があります。ただ、時制は時間と違って、客観的・物理的な概念ではありません。伝えようとしている事柄を時間の流れの中で話し手がどこに位置付けるのか、つまり、現在よりも前なのか後なのかは、話し手の意識によって決まります。このunitでは、英語の過去形が持つ「隔たり」と、助動詞willについて学習します。

2．過去形が持つ３つの「隔たり」

「過去形は、『過去の事実』や『過去の習慣』を表す」と教わります。勿論、それ自体は間違ってはいません。しかし、英語の過去形は、「時間」「事実」「心理」の面で重要な役割を担っています。それは、「隔たり」です。この感覚が身に付けば、過去形への理解がグンと深まります。

(1) 現在との時間的隔たり

現在よりも以前に起きたことを、つまり、過去の事実や習慣を表します（「現在は違うが」といった含みがあります）。

I loved you.
（君のことが好きだった）→ 今は違うけど…

There was Hiroshi's guitar room around here thirty years ago.
（30年前、この辺りには博のギター教室があった）→ 現在はないが…

(2) 現在の事実からの隔たり

現在の事実と異なる仮定や願望を、過去形が持つ距離感を利用して表します。いわゆる、仮定法過去と呼ばれているものです。

If I Mr. Ikeda had a little more knowledge of English, we would give him

some classes.
（池田さんにもう少し英語の知識があれば、授業を任せるのに）→「英語の知識が足りないので、任せられない」という意識で話している。

I wish I could see my wife again.
（もう一度、妻に会えたらなぁ）→「もう会えない」という意識で話している。

(3) 心理的な隔たり

現在形が持つ至近距離感では話していないことを表します。つまり、過去形を用いることによって、心理的距離（遠慮の気持ち）を伝えています。

Could you do me a favor?
（お願いがあるのですが）→ **Can you do me a favor?** よりも控え目なニュアンス。

I hoped that you would come.
（来てくださると思っています）→ **I hope that you will come.** よりも控え目なニュアンス。

このように、過去形に接したら、どの面での「隔たり」（時間面、事実面、心理面）なのかを意識してください。

3．未来表現

次に、未来表現について勉強しましょう。敢えて「未来表現」としたのは、英語には未来形がないからです。「未来の will があるだろ！」という反論が返ってきそうですが、will は未来形ではありません。英語では動詞の語尾を屈折（変化）させて「時」を表しますが、その語尾変化で表すことができるのは、want と wanted のように、現在と過去だけです。will は発話時（文を発するとき）の意思を表す現在形です。だから、would という過去形も存在します。未来形に過去形が存在したら、論理破綻です。尚、be going to も未来形ではありません。現時点で既に予定していることを表しています。

(1)「発話時の意思 **will**」と「予定の **be going to**」

will の本質は、発話時の意思です。「絶対にするぞ」という強い意思から、「私がするよ」という軽い意思まで、幅広く使えます。

I will never stop wanting to be a tax accountant, no matter how many years it takes.
（何年かかっても、税理士になるのを諦めないぞ）→ 強い意思。したがって、**I'll** と短縮形にならずに、明瞭に発音される。

I'll get it.
（俺が電話に出るよ）→ 軽い意思。したがって、**I'll** と短縮形になる傾向が強い。

そもそも、「するつもり」は、現在の意思でしかあり得ません。「彼女に告白するつもりだ」と言うとき、告白する時点（実際の行為）は未来であっても、その意思は現時点のものを語っています。また、willには、「だろう」という予測もあります。会話の当事者でない３人称の意思は予測するしかないので、「（あいつはするつもり）だろう」という予測の意味が生まれました。当然、これも発話時の予測です。

一方、be going toは、その形からもわかるように、to以下の方向に進行中、つまり、既に流れに乗っている（予定している）ことを表しています。be going toにも、「だろう」という予測の意味がありますが、willの予測とはニュアンスが違います。to以下の方向を予測できるということは、そうなる根拠が既に存在しているときに使われます。

(2) その他の未来表現

① **be + ing**（進行形）

進行形で「予定」を表すことができます。既に決めてあった意思が、より具体的な準備へと進んでいるときは、頭の中でやっているところを描けるからです。

We're having a farewell party for Keishiro this weekend.
（今週末、景史郎の送別会を開く予定だ）

② **will be + ing**

「することになっている」といった、既に決定された事柄を伝えるときに使われます。

We'll be waiting for you in front of the hotel.
（ホテルの前で待っています）
I'll be meeting you at the entrance.
（入口でお迎えします）

この表現は、相手に心理的負担を与えないために、話し手の「意思」としてではなく、「既に決定された事柄」として伝えるために使われます。

（注）交通機関の予定を伝えるときにも用いられます。交通機関の運行状況は、既に決定されているからです。

We will be flying over Mt. Fuji in a couple of minutes.
（あと数分で富士山上空を通過します）

③ **be to V**

この表現も、「することになっている」という予定を表しますが、第三者によって決められた予定というニュアンスを含んでいます。

The President is to make a speech at the conference.
（会議では大統領がスピーチをする予定です）

（注）**be to V** は、元来、「（神の意思によって）運命付けられている」という意味でした。そこから、第三者によって決められた予定に用いられるようになりました。尚、この **be to V** には、「予定」だけでなく、「義務」「可能」の意味もありますが、根源的なイメージは同じです。

Exercises

1 与えられた語句とイラストを参考にし、自由に語句を補いながら、過去形を用いた英文を作れ。尚、与えられた語句の中には、その形を変える必要があるものもある。また、文頭に置かれる語も小文字で記している。

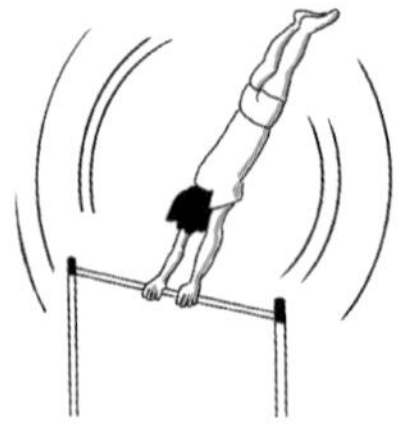

(1) [am, young, can, perform, a giant swing]

ヒント：「若ければ」という叶わぬ願望。

(2) [they, disappoint, see, the junior high school reunion]

ヒント：多くの人が思う。「再会しなければよかった」と。

(3) [will often, that coastal town, my wife]

ヒント：「過去の習慣」を述べる。意思を本質とする **will** には、同じく過去の習慣を表す **used to** よりも、「懐かしむ気持ち」が強く込められている。

(4) [Anywhere Door and Bamboo Copter]

ヒント：誰しも、「本当にあったらいいなぁ」と思ったことがあるはず。特に、遅刻しそうなときは。

(5) [will, what, know]

ヒント：・助動詞 **will** を使った依頼文。「意思」を本質とする **will** が疑問文で使われると、「依頼」に繋がる。「(そのつもりがあるなら) してくれますか？」といった感覚。
・「情報を教える」ときは **teach** ではなく、**tell** を使う。**tell** は「伝達」、**speak** は「音声」、**talk** は「コミュニケーション」、**say** は「発言内容」を基本イメージとする。

2 次の（　）内の語句を並べ換えて、適切な英文を作れ。尚、文頭に置かれるべき語も小文字で記してある。

(1) [another, beer, you, of, glass, have, won't]

ヒント：「するつもりはないの？」という勧誘文。日本語でも、「飲みに行かない？」「明日、来ない？」といった否定表現で誘うことが多い。

(2) [her, the ballpark, taking, out to, I'm] this weekend.

ヒント：「予定」を表している。既に具体的準備が進んでいるときに使われることが多い。準備や段取りが進んでいれば、頭の中で「やっているところ」を描けるから。

(3) [going, Tadashi, when and where, see, you, are, to]

ヒント：既に決めてある意思、つまり、「予定」を尋ねている。

(4) [would, he, the class reunion, said that, play the guitar, Hiroshi, at]

ヒント：「発話時の意思」を表す **will** が **that** 節で用いられている。但し、英語では動詞が登場する度に、それがいつのことなのか（現在なのか過去なのか、それとも過去の時点よりも更に過去なのか）を正確に伝えなければならない。これを、「時制の一致の法則」と言う。

(5) [those changes, not, Anju, accept, will]

ヒント：「意思」（**will**）の否定。つまり、「どうしても…しようとしない」という拒絶になる。

3 次の日本語を英訳せよ。

(1) 日本の首相が来週訪米予定です。

ヒント：・公人の予定は、第三者によって決められるのが一般的。したがって、**be to V** が使われることが多い。
・日本の首相　**the Prime Minister of Japan**

(2) 今日の午後は、墓参りへ行きます。

ヒント：・一般的に、「墓参り」は予定していることが多い。
・墓参り　**visit the grave**

(3) 誰か来たみたい。見てくるわ。

ヒント：・気配を感じてから抱いた意思。したがって、「予定」ではなく、「発話時の意思」
・見てくる　**go and see, go to see**

Unit 8　動詞の世界（3）—have が語る現在完了のネットワーク

1．はじめに

中学生の後半頃に、「現在完了は『have+ 過去分詞』で作ります。意味は、『完了・結果』『経験』『継続』です」と教わったことと思います。このあたりから、英語がわからなくなってきた人も多いことでしょう。時制（「時」を伝える表現）に関しては、非常にシンプルな構造を持つ日本語に対して、英語はかなり複雑な体系をしているからです。ただ、言語では、意味と構造（表現形式）は不可分です。意味が構造を決め、構造が意味を表します。現在完了の構造を改めて見てください。中核にあるのは have です。この have は助動詞ですが、「自己の所有空間や領域に持っている」という動詞 have と本質的に同じです。girlfriend（人）や car（物）が持っている対象なら理解できるのに、finished the homework（状況）になると、どうしてわからないのでしょうか？基本イメージはまったく同じです。「過去分詞が表す状況（finished the homework）を、今、持っている（have）」と言っているのです。つまり、話し手の焦点は「現在」にあります。だから、have を使っているのです。ただ、その対象が人や物ではなく、「終わったこと（例：夕食を食べたこと）」「経験したこと（例：留学したこと）」「現在まで行ってきたこと（例：３年間、東京に住んでいること）」などの状況なのです。「現在完了は、過去の期日を表す表現と一緒には使えない」と言われるのもこのためです。例えば、I saw her in Kobe yesterday.（昨日、神戸で彼女と会った）では過去（昨日）の出来事を述べており、話し手は現在に焦点を置けないからです。この unit では、そうした現在完了の中核イメージを学びます。

2．「完了・結果」「経験」「継続」とは

過去が現在へと繋がってくる感覚の現在完了ですが、それを分析的に表現した言葉が、「完了・結果」「経験」「継続」です。どの意味かは、文脈や常識から判断できる場合がほとんどです。例えば、一般的な日本人が、

I have taken a bath.

と言えば、「経験」とは考えにくいです。風呂に入ったことを自慢げに現在の経験

として語る人はいないからです（そんな人もいるかもしれませんが、言われた相手は引いてしまいます）。

(1) 完了・結果

過去の出来事の影響が、現在に表れていることを意識するときに使われます。

I have finished the assignments for tomorrow.
（明日の課題は終えちゃったよ）→ 例えば、「だから、飲みに行けるよ」「もう寝るよ」といった気持ち。

(2) 経験

過去の出来事が、現在の主語の立場に何らかの要素を付け加えているときに使われます。この要素にはプラス面もあれば、マイナス面もあります。

Mr. Shibusawa has played in the summer Koshien Tournament.
（渋沢先生は、夏の甲子園に出場したことがある）→ 例えば、「それほどの実績がある人だ」「だから、野球部の指導を任せたい」といった気持ち。

That guy has cheated on me several times.
（あの男は、何度も私を裏切った）→例えば、「だから、あいつは信用できない」「あいつは、そういった奴だ」といった気持ち。

(3) 継続

「完了・結果」の場合に似て、現在まで続いてきた行為や状態の影響が、現在に表れていることを意識するときに使われます。

My husband has been yelling at a sales rep for more than ten minutes.
（夫は、営業マンに10分以上喚いている）→ 例えば、「恥ずかしいから、もうやめて」「もうウンザリ」といった気持ち。

3．現在完了の否定文と疑問文

現在完了の否定文と疑問文では、一般動詞のように do/does を使いません。否定文では have not (haven't)+過去分詞、疑問文では Have S+過去分詞？となります。

Mr. Saito has not decided to marry yet.
（斎藤さんは、まだ結婚の決断をしていない）

Have you ever lashed out violently at a policeman, Mr. Honma?
（本間さん、警官に暴力を振るったことがあるのですか？）

その理由は、否定文・疑問文で用いられる do/does も、現在完了の have も共に助動詞なので、同時に使うと助動詞が連続してしまうからです。I will may should study ... が非文であることは、容易に理解できると思います。

4．現在完了と共に使われることが多い副詞（句）

現在完了では、just（ちょうど、たった今）、already（既に）、yet（まだ、もう）、ever（今までで）、never（今まで一度もない）、always（いつも）、... times（…回）などの副詞（句）がよく使われます。

Keishiro has already decided to leave her.
（景史郎は、既に彼女と別れる決心をした）

How many times has Hiroshi ever sat for the exam?
（博は何回その試験を受けたの？）

Exercises

1 次の日本語の内容に合うように、（　）内に適切な英語を入れよ。尚、短縮形や副詞が入る箇所もある。

(1) I (　　　　　) (　　　　　) (　　　　　) to the open-air bath.

（ちょうど、露天風呂に行ってきたところよ）

ヒント：「行ってきたところ」は **have been or have gone?**

(2) Hayato (　　　　　) (　　　　　) to quit that university (　　　　　).

（勇人は、まだあの大学を辞める決心をしていない）

ヒント：「まだ…でない」という意味で使われる副詞は？

(3) That couple (　　　　　) (　　　　　) (　　　　　) to each other since they had a quarrel last night.

（昨夜、口論をして以来、あの夫婦は口を聞いていない）

ヒント： **since SV ...**「…以来」は、「継続」で用いられる。

(4) (　　　　　) you (　　　　　) (　　　　　) the northern Japanese alps?

（日本の北アルプスを見たことある？）

ヒント： 「どの時点を取り出しても」という意味で使われる副詞は？

(5) The work (　　　　　) (　　　　　) (　　　　　) (　　　　　) by them.

（その仕事は、既に彼らの手で完成している）

ヒント：・現在完了の受動態の作り方は？
・「既に…」という意味で使われる副詞は？

(6) (　　　　　) you (　　　　　) goodbye to her (　　　　　)?

（もう彼女にサヨナラを言ったの？）

ヒント：「もう…？」という意味で使われる副詞は？

(7) Masafumi and Chiharu (　　　　　) (　　　　　) (　　　　　) about that psychologist.

（正史と千春は、あの心理学者への不満を言ってきた）

ヒント：行為を表す動詞が「継続」を表すときは、現在完了進行形を用いる。

2 過去のことを話題にしながら、現在に焦点がある現在完了（**have** ＋過去分詞）を用いて、次の日本語を英訳せよ。

(1) 彼が英語を話すのを聞いたことある？　まるで、ネイティブだよ。

____

ヒント：・経験を尋ねるときは、現在完了に **ever** を添えるとわかり易い。**ever** は「**any** の時間版」と考えればわかり易い。つまり、「いつの時点を取り出しても」といったニュアンス。「（今までのいつの時点でもいいから）彼が英語を話すのを聞いたことある？」と尋ねている。

・まるで…　**It's like ...**

(2) これほど無駄な会議に出たことがない。

____

ヒント：・経験を否定するときは、現在完了に **never** を添える。**never** は「**not + any** の時間版」と考えればわかり易い。つまり、「いつの時点を取り出しても…ない」と言っている。

・無駄な　**useless, unproductive**

(3) 景史郎は上海に何度も行ったことがある。

ヒント：・「行ったことがある」では、**go** を使ってはいけない。**go** は「領域外へ出るイメージ、離れていくイメージ」なので、**have gone** だと「離れてしまった状態（いない状態）」になってしまう。「行ったことがある」とは、「その場所に存在したことがある」という意味なので、存在を表す **be** 動詞を用いる。

・肯定文では **ever** を使わない。**ever** は「いつの時点を取り出しても」という意味なので、「いつの時点を取り出しても行ったことがある」では意味不明になってしまう。

・何度も　**many times**

(4) 別れてから 15 年だね。元気だった？

ヒント：・**A** 以来…　**It has been ... since A/... have passed since A**

・別れる　**break up**

・元気だった　「今までどうだった？」と考える。

(5) あの柔道家は、プロレスラー相手に 30 分以上も戦い続けている。

ヒント：・現在までの行為や動作の継続には、現在完了進行形（**have been ... ing**）を用いるのが一般的。

・柔道家　**judo master**

・プロレスラー　**(pro) wrestler**

・…と戦う　**fight with ...**

Unit 9　動詞の世界（4）— 焦点を移動させた完了形

1．はじめに

このunitでは、「過去完了」「未来完了」と呼ばれている完了形の拡大バージョンを学びます。「拡大」という表現がピンとこなければ、「移動」と言うほうが適切かもしれません。では、何が移動するのでしょうか？それは、話し手の「焦点（視点）」です。それぞれ、具体的に見ていきましょう。

2．焦点（視点）を過去に移動させると **had**

現在完了では、過去（から）の出来事を述べていながら、話し手の焦点は現在（have）にありました。過去完了では、その焦点が「過去の特定の時点」に移っただけです。ただ、話題にしている事柄が、その時点では「終わっていたこと」（完了・結果）「経験したこと」（経験）「続けてきたこと」（継続）になります。

「パーティーに到着したとき、あの女性たちは料理を平らげてしまっていた」

という文を考えてみましょう。話し手の焦点は、過去の特定の時点である「パーティーに到着したとき」にあります。ただ、「料理を平らげてしまっていた」と述べているように、その時点では既に終わっていたことを話題にしています。こうしたときに、過去完了を使うのです。形は簡単です。haveをhadにすればいいだけです。

Those women had (already) cleaned their plates when I got to the party.
その時点では既に終わっていたこと　　　　　　　話し手の焦点

となります。ここで注意すべき点があります。

His train had (already) left when Shizuka reached the station.
（静が駅に着いたとき、彼の列車は既に出てしまっていた）

とすべきところを、

His train left when Shizuka reached the station.

としたら、どうなるのでしょうか？　確かに、実際に起こり得る状況です。但し、この文の場合、聞き手には、「静が駅に着いたのとほぼ同時に、彼の列車は出た」という印象を与えてしまいます。

３．焦点（視点）を未来へ移動させると will

学校では「未来完了」という難解な用語で教わりますが、現在完了の前に「予測」を表す助動詞 will が置かれただけです。なぜ、will なのか？理由は簡単です。未来のことは予測するしかないからです。つまり、未来完了とは、話し手の焦点を「未来の特定の時点」に移したときの予測です（勿論、予測しているのは、話しているときです）。ただ、話題にしている事柄が、その時点では「終わっていること」（完了・結果）「経験したこと」（経験）「続けてきたこと」（継続）になります。

「君にこのメッセージが届く頃には、僕はニューヨークを去っていることだろう」

という文を考えてみましょう。話し手の焦点は、未来の特定の時点である「このメッセージが届く頃」です。ただ、「去っていることだろう」と述べているように、その時点では既に終わっていることを予測しています。こうしたときに、未来完了を使うのです。形は簡単、「will+ 現在完了」で OK です。

I will have (already) left New York by the time this message reaches you.
その時点では既に終わっていること　　　　　　　　　　　　話し手の焦点

となります。ここでも注意すべき点があります。

His train will have (already) left when Shizuka reaches the station.
（静が駅に着くときには、彼の列車は既に出てしまっているだろう）

とすべきところを、

His train will leave when Shizuka reaches the station.

としたら、どうなるのでしょうか？　これも、実際に起こり得る状況です。但し、この文の場合、聞き手には、「静が駅に着くのとほぼ同時に、彼の列車は出るだろう」という印象を与えてしまいます。

Exercises

1 次の日本語の内容に合うように、(　) 内に適切な英語を入れよ。

(1) I (　　　　) (　　　　) (　　　　) that oddball by chance four times if I bump into him again. What a coincidence!

(今度、あの変人に遭遇したら、４度目だよ。なんという偶然だ！)

ヒント：話し手の焦点は？　その時点での経験回数。

(2) How many times (　　　　) you (　　　　) it a go before you gave it up?

(諦めるまで何回挑戦したの？)

ヒント：話し手の焦点は？　その時点での経験回数。

(3) Junko insisted then that she (　　　　) (　　　　) (　　　　) all kinds of cakes.

(ケーキを全種類食べたわけではないと、純子はそのとき言い張った)

ヒント：話し手の焦点は？その時点での完了・結果。

(4) That athlete (　　　　) (　　　　) (　　　　) for fifteen minutes or so when he sprained his ankle.

(あのアスリートは、15分ほどランニングをしたら、足首を捻挫してしまった)

ヒント：話し手の焦点は？その時点までの継続。

(5) Masafumi (　　　　) (　　　　) (　　　　) (　　　　) as the university president around this time next year.

(来年の今頃は、正史が学長に選出されていることだろう)

ヒント：話し手の焦点は？その時点での完了・結果。

(6) That professor (　　　　) (　　　　) (　　　　) (　　　　) illogically for an hour by five o'clock.

(５時を迎えると、あの教授が訳のわからないことを話し始めてから１時間になる)

ヒント：話し手の焦点は？その時点までに継続。

2 伝えようとする２つの出来事に時間差があるとき、話し手の焦点（基準時）がいつなのか（過去なのか、未来なのか）によって、過去完了か未来完了かが決まる。その点に注意して、次の日本語を英訳せよ。

(1) 帰宅したら、玄関のカギを失くしていることに気付いた。

ヒント：・話し手の焦点は？
・…に気付く　**find (that) SV ...**
・なくす　**lose**

(2) 来年の３月で、家族が全員私の元を去ってから５年になる。

ヒント：・話し手の焦点は？
・年月が過ぎる　**pass**

(3) 晃代が話し始めてから数分で、あるトルコ人の男性が割り込んできた。

ヒント：・話し手の焦点は？
・（話に）割り込む　**cut in**

(4) あなたがブラジルに戻って来る頃には、状況は変わっているわ。

ヒント：・話し手の焦点は？
・状況　**things**

(5) 去年の同窓会で話したときには、彼女は２回離婚していた。

ヒント：・話し手の焦点は？
・同窓会　**class reunion**

(6) 今度やったら、3回目の裏切りよ。

ヒント：・話し手の焦点は？
・…を裏切る **be disloyal to ...**

Unit 10　動詞の世界（5）―「思い」を語る仮定法

1．はじめに

人の頭の中には、「現実世界」と「仮想世界」という２つの世界が存在しています。そして、言語表現の半分以上が、「仮想世界」を描いたものではないでしょうか。それは、怒り、悲しみ、後悔、無念、賞賛など、諸々の「思い」を裏から表現するのが人間の性（さが）だからです。「もっとお金があれば…」「あんな優しい人が恋人だったら…」「あのとき…していれば」なんていう思いは、誰しもよく抱くはずです。この裏街道の担当者が、「仮定法」です。ここでは、その基本形である「仮定法過去」と「仮定法過去完了」を中心に学びます。

2．「今はそうじゃないんだけど…」という思いで語る仮定法過去

「過去」という言葉が使われていますが、過去の出来事を述べているのではありません。過去形の箇所でも述べましたが、英語では、現実からのズレも過去形を使って表します。現在から時間的に離れていることを表す過去形のイメージを利用して、現在の事実から離れていることを、つまり、「今はそうじゃないんだけど…」という思いを、過去形に託して表しているのです。例えば、

I wish I had more talent.
（もっと才能があればなぁ）

では、「ああ、自分には才能が足りない」という話し手の思いが滲み出ています。また、

If that country can keep its word, we will sign the treaty.
（あの国が約束を守れるのなら、条約に調印しよう）

では、あの国が約束を守る可能性はあると話し手は考えていますが、

If that country could keep its word, we would sign the treaty.
（あの国が約束を守れるのなら、条約に調印するのだけど）

では、あの国は約束を守れないという思いを、話し手は強く抱いています。こうしたとき、つまり、「現実とは異なる、またはその可能性が高い」と思うときに仮定法過去を使います。

作り方は簡単。願望を述べたいのであれば、I wish SV ... の V を過去形にする

だけでOKです。また、「もし…なら」と仮定するのであれば、if節（条件節）の中で動詞の過去形を使い、「…だろう」（帰結節）の部分でも、would/could/mightなど、助動詞の過去形を使えばいいだけです。

尚、ifの使用は、必須ではありません。文の冗長さを嫌うため、ifなしのほうが圧倒的に多く使われます。では、どこで仮定法だと見抜くのでしょうか？そのポイントは、would/could/mightといった助動詞の過去形です。例えば、会話の相手に対して、

I wouldn't do that.
（俺ならそんなことはしないよ）

とだけ言えば、if I were you（俺が君なら）の部分は文脈上明白です。

また、仮定法では、主語がI/he/ she /itであっても、be動詞はwereを使うのがフォーマルです。これは人称までも一致させないことによって、現実からのズレを強調したい気持ちがあるからです。現在では、wasのほうが多く使われますが、if it were not for ...（…がなければ）やif I were you（俺がお前なら）などは、擬古体によるイディオム化の現象によって、wereのほうが根強いです。

3．「あのときはそうじゃなかったんだけど…」という思いで語る仮定法過去完了

では、「あのとき会議で発言すればよかった」「敦のように誠実に生きていればなぁ」と、過去の事実とは異なる思いを表現したいときはどうすればいいのでしょうか。そのときは、過去形をもう1つバックシフトさせるだけでOKです。そうです、過去完了形（had+過去分詞）を使うのです。例えば、上の日本語だと、

I wish I had spoken out at the meeting.

I wish I had lived an honest life like Atsushi.

となります。ifを用いた表現でも同じです。

If you had told him the truth, he would have left here.
（あなたが彼に真実を話していたら、彼はここからいなくなっていたでしょう）

If I had been in your shoes, I wouldn't have shot him.
（君の立場にいたら、俺は撃たなかっただろう）

—If I hadn't (shot him), they could have been killed.
（私が撃たなかったら、彼らは殺されていた可能性がありますよ）

といったように。もちろん、仮定法過去完了も、「would/could/ might have+ 過去分詞」の部分だけで表現できます。上の文では、文脈上明白な If I hadn't (shot him) を省略して、They could have been killed. だけで十分伝わります。

４．仮定法未来と仮定法現在

仮定法には、「仮定法未来」「仮定法現在」と呼ばれているものもあります。ただ、名称は違っても、話し手が描く仮想世界（反事実・非事実）という点では、変わりありません。

(1) 仮定法未来

学校で「仮定法未来」と教わるこの表現は、「仮定法過去の一種」とも言えます。「未来の実現可能性の乏しい事柄を仮定する」と言われていますが、仮定法過去との違いは微妙です。例えば、「鳥だったら」（仮定法過去）と「鳥になったら」（仮定法未来）とでは、ほとんど同じです。また、仮定法未来では were を使いますが、これも仮定法過去と同じです。ただ、細かいニュアンスの差を言えば、仮定法未来では to V（to 不定詞）を使う点から見ても、話し手の意識は未来に向けられています。作り方は、

If he should come tomorrow, give this to him.
（万が一彼が明日来たら、これを渡してくれ）

If she were to be here again, I would do anything.
（彼女が再び現れてくれるなら、僕は何でもするだろう）

のように、if 節（条件節）の中で should か were to を使います。どちらも実現可能性の乏しいことを仮定しますが、常識や科学ではあり得ないことを想定するときは、通常、were to が使用されます。また、should を用いた場合は、もう一方の文（帰結節）では、助動詞は過去形でも現在形でも構いません。また、上の例文のように、命令文でも OK です。

(2) 仮定法現在

if need be（必要なら）/God bless you!（神の祝福があらんことを！）などの慣用表現を除けば、アメリカ英語において、次の形で残存しています。

Mr. Myojo insisted that Mr. Yoshida attend the meeting in Osaka.
（明城先生は、吉田先生が大阪での会議に出席すべきだと言い張った）

She suggested that the meeting be put off.
（彼女は会議の延期を提案した）

つまり、「要請・主張・命令・提案・助言」等を表す動詞が、that 節を目的語に取るときに、その節中で動詞の原形が使われます。この原形を「仮定法現在」と呼びます。では、なぜこれが仮定法なのでしょうか。実は、動詞の原形は、「現実世界」を表していません。例えば、

Study harder, Hiroshi.
（博、もっと真面目に勉強しなさい）

と、命令文では文頭に動詞の原形が置かれます。その理由は、相手に命令するときは、現実と反対のことを命じるからです。お母さんは、息子が勉強していないと思っているから、「勉強しなさい」と命令しているのです。要求や提案も同じです。理想と現実が違っていると思うときに、要求や提案は行われます。だから、非現実世界（仮想世界）を表す原形が使われるのです。

5．さまざまな仮定法表現

その他、いくつかの仮定法表現を紹介しましょう。使いこなすには、多くの問題に取り組まなければなりません。

If only Kaoru were with me! （仮定法過去）
（かおるが一緒にいてくれさえすれば）

If only I had met you in my youth! （仮定法過去完了）
（若いときに、君に出会ってさえいれば）

Hideyuki talks as if he were everyone's crush. （仮定法過去）
（英幸は、自分がモテモテのような口ぶりだ）

Hideyuki talks as if he had been everyone's crush. （仮定法過去完了）
（英幸は、自分がモテモテだったような口ぶりだ）

Hirofumi <u>would rather</u> she <u>were</u> not at the meeting. （仮定法過去）
（博史は、彼女が会議にいなければいいなあと思っている）

Mr. Yamada <u>would rather</u> he <u>had not asked</u> that accountant to file a tax return. （仮定法過去完了）
（山田さんは、あの税理士に確定申告を頼まなければよかったと思っている）

<u>It's time</u> you <u>gave up</u> studying English, Kenzo. （仮定法過去）
（賢三、もう英語の勉強は諦める頃だよ）

Exercises

1 次の日本語の内容に合うように、(　) 内に適切な語を入れよ。

(1) If I (　　　　　) the guy, I (　　　　　) attend the class reunion.

(私がアイツなら、同窓会には出ないだろう)

ヒント：「私がアイツなら」は現在の反事実 **or** 過去の反事実？

(2) I wish my son (　　　　　) (　　　　　) harder when he (　　　　　) a high school student.

(息子が高校時代にもっと勉強していたらなぁ)

ヒント：「勉強していたら」は現在の反事実 **or** 過去の反事実？

(3) If only my wife (　　　　　) (　　　　　) (　　　　　) that way then!

(あのとき、妻があんなふうにさえ言わなければ)

ヒント：「あのとき、言わなければ」は現在の反事実 **or** 過去の反事実？

(4) If I (　　　　　) (　　　　　) the flight, I (　　　　　) (　　　　　) alive now.

(あの飛行機に乗っていたら、生きて今ここにいないだろう)

ヒント：・「乗っていたら」は現在の反事実 **or** 過去の反事実？
・「今ここにいない」は現在の反事実 **or** 過去の反事実？

(5) That professor talks (　　　　　) (　　　　　) he (　　　　　) a singer-songwriter.

(あの教授は、まるで自分がシンガーソングライターのような口ぶりだ)

ヒント：「シンガーソングライターのような」は現在の反事実 **or** 過去の反事実？

2 例文にあるように、仮定法は倒置によっても表すことができる。倒置による仮定法では、**were / had / should** が必ず条件節（もし…なら）の先頭に置かれる。それを用いて、次の日本語の内容に合うように、与えられた語句を使い英訳せよ。尚、与えられた語句の順序を変えてはいけない。

（例）Were I you (= If I were you), I would quit such a strenuous job.

（私が君なら、そんなきつい仕事は辞めるね）

Had he known the truth (= If he had known the truth), he could have held back.

（彼が真実を知っていたら、思い止まることができただろう）

(1) 祖母からの経済的援助がなければ、彼はあの大学に通えないだろう。

（**were, it, for, could not**）

ヒント： **if it were not for ...**（仮定法過去）の倒置表現。これは、**It is for his grandmother's financial backing that he can go to that university.**（彼があの大学に通えるのは、祖母からの経済的援助のお陰だ）という **cleft sentence**（分裂文→学校では、「強調構文」という名称で教えられている）の、**It is for his grandmother's financial backing** の部分が、反事実を表す仮定法として用いられ、**If it were not for his grandmother's financial backing** という形になったもの。つまり、「彼があの大学に通えるのは、祖母からの経済的援助のお陰だ（**for his grandmother's financial backing**）」→「祖母からの経済的援助がなければ、彼はあの大学に通えないだろう」となる。

(2) 君のあの言葉がなかったら、僕は命を落としていたかもしれない。

（**it, not, been, lose**）

ヒント： **if it had not been for ...**（仮定法過去完了）の倒置表現。考え方は **(1)** と同じ。尚、**(1) (2)** のような倒置形は形式張った表現であり、口語では改まった場面を除けばほとんど使われない。しかし、書き言葉では、擬古体によるイディオム化の現象が見られ、**were it not for/had it not been for** は、**if it were not for/if it had not been for** の数倍の頻度で使用されている。

(3) 彼にもっと勇気があれば、あの女上司に抵抗していただろう。

（**he, fought against, that female boss, more courageous**）

ヒント： **if he had been more courageous**（仮定法過去完了）の倒置表現。

(4) 万が一、佳子が来たら、真実を伝えてくれ。

(**should**, **tell**)

ヒント：**If Yoshiko should come here**（仮定法未来）の倒置表現。

3 次の日本語を、**if** を用いずに英訳せよ。

(1) 300 年前だったら、明城先生の物理学理論は受け入れられていただろう。

ヒント：・「**300** 年前」が条件節（**if ...**）の代わりをしてくれる。
・受け入れられていただろう → 過去の反事実。

(2) あの人のことは、もう忘れてもいい頃よ。

ヒント：・もう…する頃だ　**It's time SV**（過去形）**...**
・…を忘れる　**get over ...**

(3) もう少し英語の知識があれば、池田氏はここの教員になれたのに。

ヒント：・**A** があれば　**with A**
・教員になれたのに → 過去の反事実

(4) 明夫は早々に帰宅した。そうでなければ、奥さんに叱られていただろう。

ヒント：・そうでなければ…　**otherwise ...**
・叱る　**tell off**

(5) 吉田先生はもっと授業をするべきだと、明城先生は言い張った。

ヒント：・言い張る　**insist (that) SV**（原形）→ 仮定法現在
・授業をする　**give/teach a lesson**

Unit 11　文の種類（1）— 否定表現が多彩な英語

1．はじめに

肯定文に勝るとも劣らない頻度の「否定文」について学びましょう。「あの人から連絡は来なかったわ」「明日、学校に行きたくない」「駆けっこでは、いつもあいつに勝てなかった」など、日常生活において否定文を使わない日はありません。特に、白黒肯否を曖昧にしがちな日本語文化に対して、それを明確にする傾向がある英語文化では、否定表現は多種多様です。この unit では、先ずは not を使った否定文の基本を確認し、その後、no を含んだ「全部否定」と、ゼロでもすべてでもない「部分否定」について学びます。

2．not を使った「…でない」

最初に学習する否定文ですね。作り方は３つに分けることができます。

(1) 助動詞（can, will, should, etc.）を使った文

助動詞の直後に not を置くだけで OK です。

She will not (won't) stand by me for the rest of my life.
（私の残りの人生、彼女は側にいてくれないだろう）

The dean could not (couldn't) talk back to the female professor.
（学部長は、その女性教授に口答えができなかった）

(2) be 動詞を使った文

これも助動詞の場合と同じです。be 動詞の直後に not を置きます。

She is not (isn't) good at controlling her emotions.
（彼女は感情のコントロールが上手くできない）

They were not (weren't) celebrities.
（彼らはセレブではなかった）

(3) 一般動詞を使った文

一般動詞の場合は、動詞の前に do/does/did を置いて、その後ろに not を加えます。ただ、否定文や疑問文で使われる do/does/did は助動詞なので、結局は、助動詞のときと同じです。

I do not (don't) like being treated like her younger brother.
（彼女の弟のような扱いは受けたくない）

That assistant did not (didn't) invite her boss to the wedding ceremony.
（あの助手は、上司を結婚式に呼ばなかった）

(4) **not** の作用域（打ち消している部分）は右側

学校では、「is の否定形は is not (短縮形は isn't), will の否定形は will not (短縮形は won't) です」と教わるので、not は is や will を否定しているように思い込んでしまいますが、それは間違いです。実は、not は右側を否定しています。例えば、He did not hurt her feelings on purpose. の場合 , 通常、not が否定しているのは下線部になります。

① **He did not hurt her feelings on purpose.**

つまり、not は「意図的に彼女の気持ちを傷付けた」の部分を打ち消しています。「意図的に彼女の気持ちを傷付けたのではない → 過って傷付けてしまった」という意味になります。それに対して、on purpose の部分が not の左側に置かれた On purpose, he did not hurt her feelings. の場合、not が否定しているのは下線部になります。

② **On purpose, he did not hurt her feelings.**

つまり、not は「彼女の気持ちを傷付けた」の部分を打ち消しています。「彼女の気持ちを傷付けなかった。それは意図的にそうしたのだ」という意味になります。おわかりですね？　①では、「意図的でないにせよ、彼女の気持ちを傷付けた」のであり、②では、「意図的に、彼女の気持ちを傷付けなかった」のです。無論、右側のどこまでを否定しているのかは、文の意味から判断してください。例えば、

Not he but I am to blame.
（彼ではなく、私の責任です）

では、not が打ち消しているのは he だけです。

3．全部を否定するのに楽な英語

英語は主語や目的語の名詞の前に no を置いて、ゼロを表すことができます。この no は名詞を修飾する形容詞であり、その名詞をゼロにします。簡単に言えば、「no 名詞」は「ゼロ×名詞」だと考えてください。ゼロに何を掛けてもゼロになるように、可算名詞であれ不可算名詞であれ、単数形であれ複数形であれ、ゼロ（その名詞はまったくない）となります。

My husband has no friend(s) to talk with.
（夫には話せる友人はゼロ → 話せる友人がいない）

No alcohol is allowed here.
（ここで許可されているアルコールはゼロ → アルコールは禁止です）

日本語では、「昨日、取った水分はゼロ」「その部屋で見かけた人はゼロ」なんていう表現は一般的ではありません。日本語の否定文では、動詞もしくは形容動詞を打ち消すからです。したがって、「昨日、水分を取らなかった」「その部屋では誰も見かけなかった」と表現します。勿論、英語でも、I didn't drink any water yesterday./I didn't see anyone in the room. と言えます。でも、同時に、

I drank no water yesterday.
I saw no one in the room.

とも言えるのです。この no 名詞はとても強い否定です。特に、no 単数名詞は「1つとしてない」というニュアンスなのですから。

そして、もう1つ重要なことは、no を含んだ語が単独で代名詞や副詞として使われている点です。nobody/nothing/none/nowhere などがその例です。

尚、not + any で no とほぼ同意になります。any は「どんな（どれを取っても）」という意味なので、それを否定すると、「どんな…も not」、つまり、ゼロになるからです。

I didn't see anyone today.
（今日はどんな人にも会わなかった → 誰にも会わなかった）

Hiroshi doesn't have anything to talk about.
（博にはどんな話題もない → 博には話題がまったくない）

となります。

4．部分否定に注意

部分否定とは、「一部肯定、一部否定」です。つまり、100 でもゼロでもないということです。日本語で例を挙げると、「全員が招待されたわけではなかった（招待された者もいれば、されなかった者もいる）「愛情だけですべてが解決できるとは限らない（解決できる場合もあれば、できない場合もある）」となります。英語では not の右側に all/every/always/necessarily/quite/completely/entirely/totally/altogether など、「すべて」「いつも」「まったく」「全面的に」といった語が置かれます。ここで注意すべきは、not の右側だという点です。左側だと、全部否定なのか、部分否定なのかが紛らわしくなるからです。これは先述した「not は右側を否定する」という点と関係します。例えば、

The rich are always not happy.

だと、not が打ち消している部分は happy だけなので、「幸せでないのは、金持ちにはいつものことだ → 金持ちはいつも幸せではない」という全部否定になってしまいます。また、

All the staff members did not come to the party.

でも、not が打ち消している部分は come to the party なので、「パーティーに来なかった社員は全員だ → パーティーに来た社員はいなかった」という全部否定なってしまいます。これらの表現を部分否定にしたければ、always/all を not の右側に置く必要があります。つまり、

The rich are not always happy.
（金持ちは、いつも幸せというのではない →
金持ちは、いつも幸せとは限らない）

Not all the staff members came to the party.
（社員全員がパーティーに来たのではない → 社員全員がパーティーに来たわけではない）

となります。慣れるまでは少し難しく感じるかもしれませんが、「部分否定は not all/every/always」と覚えておけば OK です。

Exercises

1 次の英文を、**not** を使った否定文にせよ。

(1) Akiko is a common Japanese name now.

____

ヒント： **be** 動詞における **not** の位置は？

(2) Junichi and Hiroshi have been getting along great together recently.

____

ヒント：・完了形における **not** の位置は？
・**get along great together**　仲がいい

(3) My husband's car was badly damaged.

____

ヒント：・受動態における **not** の位置は？
・**badly**　とても

(4) You must eat and drink in this room.

____

ヒント：助動詞における **not** の位置は？

(5) Sayuri had her chocolate stolen by her mother.

____

ヒント：この **had** は一般動詞。過去完了ではない。

(6) Mr. Honma had already knocked the policemen to their knees when Mr. Yasuda reached there.

ヒント：・過去完了における **not** の位置は？
・「まだ…でない」で使われる副詞は？
・**knock A to A's knees**　**A** を叩きのめす

2 次の日本語に合うように、(　) 内に適切な否定詞を入れよ。

(1) (　　　　　) more, (　　　　　) less.

(これ以上でも、これ以下でもない)

ヒント：「ゼロ」を表す語は？

(2) I can wait for you (　　　　　) longer.

(もうこれ以上、あなたを待てないわ)

ヒント： **not + any longer** と言い換えることも可能。

(3) Mr. Yoshida was found (　　　　　) in Kokura.

(吉田先生は、小倉のどこにもいなかった)

ヒント：「どこにも…ない」という意味を表す語は？

(4) (　　　　　) will understand my feelings.

(誰も僕の気持ちをわかってくれないだろう)

ヒント：「誰も…ない」という意味を表す語は？

(5) Her sister is (　　　　　) kind nor beautiful.

(彼女の姉は優しくも美しくもない)

ヒント： **nor** と相関的に用いられ、両者とも否定する語は？

(6) (　　　　　) (　　　　　), thanks.

(もう十分です。ありがとう)

ヒント：追加やおかわりを断るときに使われることが多い。

3 次の日本語を英訳せよ。

(1) 彼ら全員が、その提案に反対しているわけではない。

ヒント：・**all** と **not** の位置関係は？
・**be against/be opposed to A**　**A** に反対している

(2) 景史郎は、意図的に彼女の気持ちを傷付けたのではない。

ヒント：・「意図的に」と **not** の位置関係は？
・意図的に　**deliberately/intentionally/on purpose**

(3) 斎藤さんは、すべての会員一人一人と会ったわけではなかった。

ヒント：・**every** と **not** の位置関係は？
・一人（つ）一人（つ）に焦点を置きながら「すべて」と言う場合は、**all** よりも **every** のほうが適切。

(4) ここの規則を完全に理解したわけではない。

ヒント：・**completely/totally/perfectly, etc.** と **not** の位置関係は？
・ここの規則　**the rules here**

Unit 12 文の種類（2）―英語は倒置で疑問を伝える

1．はじめに

最後のテーマは、「疑問文」です。「…ではない」という否定文同様、「…ですか？」と相手に疑問をぶつけるのも、日常生活では極めて頻度の高い表現です。そして、疑問文にも、「否定疑問」「付加疑問」「wh 疑問文」「あいづち疑問文」など、いくつかの種類があります。ここでは、それらのポイントを簡潔に紹介します。

2．英語は倒置で疑問を伝える

Are you a student?
Can you swim?

のように、英語では、主語と be 動詞 / 助動詞の語順を入れ替えて疑問文を作ります。「どうして順番をひっくり返すの？」と思った人もいるはずです。でも、この入れ替え（倒置）は仕方ないのです。なぜなら、英語には、日本語のように、

泳げます → 泳げますか？

と、文尾に付けて疑問の気持ちを表す「か」（終助詞）に相当するものがないからです。勿論、

You are a student?
You can swim?

と平叙文のままで、文尾のイントネーションを上げることによって疑問文にすることも可能です。でも、イントネーションだけでは聞き間違いのリスクもあるため、“Are you a student?” “Can you swim?” といった倒置で疑問を明確にするのです。

また、疑問文は相手に答えを委ねる点で、程度の差はあれ、話し手には感情の不安定さが伴います。つまり、語順の倒置は、こうした感情の不安定さを表しているとも言えます。

3．実は、一般動詞の疑問文も助動詞倒置

主語・動詞の倒置は、be 動詞と助動詞のときです。「一般動詞」と呼ばれているそれ以外の動詞では、do/does を使います。その理由は、be 動詞型倒置だと、例えば、

目的語を取る他動詞の場合、

Megumi and the man enjoy living together in Nagoya.
（めぐみとその男性は、名古屋での共同生活を楽しんでいる）

という英文が、

***Enjoy Megumi and the man living together in Nagoya.**

となってしまい、命令文との区別がつきにくくなるからです。そこで、一般動詞のときは助動詞 do/does を使いますが、実は、これも倒置なのです。do/does を主語の前に置くのですから。では、なぜ do/does を使うのでしょうか？　理由は簡単です。do の本来の意味を考えてください。「する」ですね。Do you eat/drive/buy ...? (食事する / 運転する / 買い物する？) と聞いているだけです。

４．感情豊かな否定疑問

疑問には気持ちの揺れが込められていますが、否定で疑問を発するときは、その気持ちが更に大きくなります。「はぁ？　来ないの？」「どうして、真面目にできないんだ？」「好きじゃなかったの？」なんて言葉には、驚き・怒り・心外などの感情が色濃く表れています。作り方は簡単です。肯定疑問に not を加えるだけで出来上がりです。

Isn't the story fishy?
（その話、怪しくないのか？）

Can't you believe me?
（俺を信じられないのか？）

Don't you think that money-making scheme smells like a rat?
（その儲け話、胡散臭いと思わないかい？）

尚、否定疑問では、応答に注意する必要があります。日本語と逆になる場合があるからです。例えば、日本語では、

純子：このレアチーズケーキ、好きじゃないの？
敦子：① いいえ、好きよ。
　　　② そうなの。好きじゃないの。

となります。それに対して、英語では、

Junko: Don't you like this raw cheesecake?
Atsuko: ① Yes, I do. I love it.
② No, I don't.

となります。つまり、英語では、「好き？」と聞かれても、「好きじゃないの？」と聞かれても、「好き」なら常に yes、「好きじゃない」のなら常に no と答えなければなりません。

5．**wh** 疑問文の特徴

最後に、疑問文の中で最も使用頻度の高い wh 疑問文についてです。wh とは疑問詞のことで、「いつ」「どこで」「誰が」「何を」「どうして」等、様々な情報を引き出すときに使われます。学校では、「5W1H」」という言葉で教わったはずです。日本語では、

あの子は神戸で誰に会ったの？
秀光は結婚式で何をやらかしたの？
あなたが突然いなくなったのは、どうして？

といったように、疑問詞は文中でも文尾でも OK です。これも日本語には、「が」「を」といった主格（主語）や目的格（目的語）を教えてくれる助詞（格助詞）があるからです。

一方、英語では、疑問詞は必ず文の先頭に置いて、疑問文であることを明確にします。なぜなら、

Did the girl see who ...?

といった語順にしてしまうと、英語では関係代名詞にも疑問詞を使うため、疑問文のつもりで疑問詞を文中に入れると、関係代名詞との区別がつきにくくなってしまうからです。したがって、

wh 疑問文では、**wh** は必ず文頭へ

という鉄則を忘れないでください。

では、Exercises に取り組みましょう。「付加疑問文」や「あいづち疑問文」にも触れています。

Exercises

1 例文を参考にして、次の英文の下線部が答えの中心になる疑問文を作れ。

（例）**I was in Niigata.**
—Where were you?

(1) Hideyuki paid no more than five hundred yen.

ヒント：・「金額」「程度」「量」などを尋ねる疑問詞は？
・**no more than ...**　…しか

(2) Hiroshi teaches bookkeeping at our school.

ヒント：・下線部が答えの中心ということは、「職業」を聞いている。「何をしていますか？」と尋ねる。「する」は **do** だが、この **do** は一般動詞。尚、職業は安定した状況なので（倒産やリストラもあるが）、現在単純形（学校で現在形として教わる形）で表すこともできる。
・疑問詞が目的語の場合でも（ここでは **what** が **teach** の目的語）、文頭に置かれる。

(3) It's about five hundred meters from here to the station.

ヒント：・「距離」を尋ねる疑問詞は？
・**It's** は **It is** の短縮形。この **It** は、「時間」「距離」「天候」などを表すときに用いる **it**（「非人称」の **it** と呼ばれている）

(4) Everyone stopped asking Akio to go for a drink more than a year ago.

ヒント：・「時」を尋ねる疑問詞は？
・**stop** は一般動詞

(5) His train leaves in ten minutes.

ヒント：・**in ...**（時間）で「時間の経過」を表す。つまり、「…経ったら」という意味。ここでの前置詞 **in** は「時間枠」を表している。

・「あとどれくらいで」と尋ねる疑問詞は？

・**leave** は一般動詞

2 例文を参考にして、次の２文を１つに繋げ。

（例）**He asked Yoko / How old are you?**（**Yoko** と **you** は同一人物を指す）

—He asked Yoko how old she was.

(1) Masafumi didn't know/Why is Chiharu angry?

ヒント：「なぜ千春が怒っているのか、正史にはわからなかった」という意味。「なぜ千春が怒っているのか」の部分が **SVO** の **O** になっている。但し、**why** 節中の時制と語順に注意すること。

(2) Nobody understood/What is Mr. Myojo trying to say?

ヒント：「明城先生が何を言おうとしているのか、誰にもわからなかった」という意味。「明城先生が何を言おうとしているのか」の部分が **SVO** の **O** になっている。但し、**what** 節中の時制・語順に注意すること。

(3) The beautiful Chinese woman asked me/When will you go back to Japan?
(me と **you** は同一人物 **)**

ヒント：「美しい中国人女性が、いつ日本に帰るのと私に聞いた」という意味。「いつ日本に帰るの」の部分が **SVO** の **O** になっている。但し、**when** 節中の人称・時制・語順に注意すること。

（注）**(1)** ～ **(3)** のポイントは間接疑問文。間接疑問文とは、疑問文を含んではいるが、それが他の文に組み込まれているため、直接に尋ねる形になっていないものをいう。したがって、文尾に疑問符（？）は不要。間接疑問文の中では、「人称」「時制」「語順」の３つに注意を払わなければならない。

3 「いつ」「どこで」「誰が」「何を」「なぜ」などの情報を求める **wh** 疑問文は、日本語と英語とでは大きな違いがある。日本語では、「彼はあのとき何を言ったの？」「あんなことをしたのは誰だ？」と、**wh** は文中や文尾に置くこともできるが、英語では、　　 の部分は必ず文頭に置かなければならない。つまり、先ず **wh** を明示し、その後の文を倒置によって疑問形にする。但し、「誰が」「何が」のように、**wh** が主語になっているときは、倒置は起きない。**Who** や **What** 自体が主語になっているため、その後に倒置すべき主語が存在しないからである。例文を参考にして、次の日本語を英訳せよ。

（例）**What did she eat this morning?**（今朝、彼女は何を食べたの？）
　　　疑問文型倒置
　　Why is he angry?（彼はなぜ怒っているの？）
　　　疑問文型倒置
　　Who told you the truth?（君に真実を話したのは誰なんだい？）
　　S　V

(1) 彼の家族に何が起きたの？

ヒント：**A** に起きる　**happen to A**

(2) あの医者は車を何台持っているんだい？

ヒント：**A** をいくつ…？ **How many A**（複数名詞）**…?**

(3) どうやってここまで来たの？

ヒント：どうやって…？ **How …?**

(4) 彼が選んだのはどちらだ？　リオか、それとも、ニューヨークか？

ヒント：どちらを…？ **Which …?**

4 「…ですよね？」と相手に確認や同意を求める疑問文は、「付加疑問文」と呼ばれている。話し手の自信の度合はイントネーションによって異なるが、最終的な選択を相手に委ねる点で、この疑問文には「肯定」と「否定」の両方が存在する。付加の部分は添えるような感覚なので、主語と同じ語を繰り返すのではなく、それを代名詞（**he, she, it, they etc.**）で軽く受け流すのがポイントである。例文を参考にして、次の英文を付加疑問文にせよ。

（例）**His wife was gracious, wasn't she?**（彼の奥さんは凛としていたよね？）
Keishiro fought honorably, didn't he?（景史郎は潔く戦ったよね？）
The professor can't say anything to her, can he?
（その先生、彼女に何も言えないよね？）

(1) Akio doesn't work at all.

ヒント：**not ... at all**　全部の点において…でない → まったく…でない（文否定。したがって、付加の部分は肯定になる）

(2) There were few students in the room.

ヒント：**few A**（複数名詞）**A** はほとんどない（文否定。したがって、付加の部分は肯定になる）

(3) Not surprisingly, Kenzo got the sack.

ヒント：・**not surprisingly**　当然（文否定ではない。したがって、付加の部分は否定になる）
・**get the sack**　クビになる

5 「へぇ、そうなの？」と会話を円滑にするための軽いあいづちも、疑問文の形で表す。例文を参考にして、次の英文に対するあいづち疑問文を作れ。

（例）**I was in Shanghai last week.**
— **Oh, were you?**

Masafumi doesn't like working overtime.
— **Oh, doesn't he?**

Hayato can be an ace here.
— **Oh, can he?**

(1) The P.E. teacher always makes a sour face.

（例の体育の先生は、いつも苦虫を噛み潰したような顔をしている）

—

(2) I wanted to see that Brazilian flight attendant again.

（あのブラジルの客室乗務員にもう一度会いたかった）

—

(3) Yasuo can't make a decision on anything.

（康男は何も決められない）

—

Note

【このテキストの作成者】

永本
(Part II)

イアン
(Part I)

町田
(Part I)

八木
(Part I)

霜田
(Part I)

加藤
(編集 ①)

中田
(編集 ②)

湯川
(イラストレーター)

Dear Class Drop Everything And Read <Second Edition> [B-968]
楽しい英語の世界へようこそ【改訂新版】

1 刷 2024年 2月 20日

著 者 永本 義弘 Nagamoto Yoshihiro
町田 純子 Machida Junko
八木 茂那子 Yagi Monako
霜田 敦子 Atsuko Shimoda
イアン・エルズワース Ian E. Ellsworth

発行者 南雲 一範 Kazunori Nagumo
発行所 株式会社 南雲堂
〒162-0801 東京都新宿区山吹町361
NAN'UN-DO Co., Ltd.
361 Yamabuki-cho, Shinjuku-ku, Tokyo 162-0801, Japan
振替口座 : 00160-0-46863
TEL: 03-3268-2311（営業部：学校関係）
03-3268-2384（営業部：書店関係）
03-3268-2387（編集部）
FAX: 03-3269-2486

編集者 加藤 敦

製 版 KA

イラスト ゆかわれい（表紙・本文）
雨宮麗恩（Unit 1 p. 8）
埼玉工業大学 オリジナルキャラクター「フカニャン」
（Reading Sections アイコン）

装 丁 Nスタジオ

検 印 省 略

コード ISBN 978-4-523-17968-9 C0082

Printed in Japan

E-mail nanundo@post.email.ne.jp
URL https://www.nanun-do.co.jp/